Lord
of
Long Beach

Lord

of

Long Beach

A GANGSTER'S JOURNEY OF FAITH

AUGUST HUNTER

Edited by Dean A. Schiffman

2010 Published by Lulu.com
Raleigh, NC

Lord of Long Beach—A Gangster's Journey of Faith/
August Hunter, Edited by Dean A. Schiffman

ISBN 978-0-557-54656-5

Contact—
Authors@LordofLongBeach.com

www.LordofLongBeach.com

Cover design—Erin Gibbons, The Designory
Contemporary Hunter photography—Lauren Radack

LLB927

To the men and women of California's jails and prisons

Who is he, this King of glory?
The Lord Almighty—he is the King of glory.

Psalm 24

Contents

Content Contributed by Other Than August Hunter

Editor's note

I met and grew to know August Hunter during 2002-2004, about the time that (unknown to me) his friend Tracy Brown was viciously gunned down in front of him. During that time, Hunter and I were both regularly visiting San Diego's Donovan State Prison, he as a former gang leader turned prison pastor and I as a volunteer in Donovan's chapel program. Hunter's base of operation for his ministry at Donovan Prison was his pastor's position at the Rock Church, a thriving San Diego megachurch.

Hunter, I observed, was a powerfully-built man in his early forties. He always walked unhurriedly through the prison complex with a slight limp. As we talked more, I experienced Hunter's discerning nature, high intelligence, genuine faith and affability. He sometimes spoke of his father being a pastor, but always did so with a sense of emotional pain.

In 2008 I wrote an article about Hunter for *San Diego Lawyer* magazine which described his remarkable journey from young gangbanger, to prison inmate, to mature gangster and finally to a renewed man in San Diego ministering to the inmates at Donovan Prison. The article created a stir in Hunter's life and among some of the current and former gangsters in Long Beach, California, Hunter's base of operation during his days in the gangs.

When the magazine article proved to be a good development, Hunter and I began talking about writing a book together. That was about the time Hunter had been scheduled for hip-replacement surgery. Shortly after Hunter's surgery, I purchased an inexpensive DVD camcorder. Our idea was to use Hunter's recuperation time for me to interview Hunter about his life. From March through September of 2008, Hunter and I recorded and transcribed twenty-two hours of his life's story in a simple conversational format, covering Hunter's life from childhood to the present. I was astounded at what I heard during the interviews. I felt that based on circumstances alone, Hunter's story was amazing; but I also knew that as a story of faith, it was invaluable.

In July of 2008—in the middle of our interview effort—Hunter's father died in New Orleans (accordingly, our readers should not be confused by Hunter's references to his father in both the present and past tenses). Shortly thereafter I made my first trip to Hunter's old neighborhood in Long Beach, when Hunter and I made a hospital visit to his friend Michael Brown, whose street name was One Round. The following September, Hunter and his fiancée Becky were married. Hunter and I finished our interviews by talking firsthand with several of the book's characters, including Henry Pirelli at Calicinto Ranch, prison inmate C. Zachary Brewster, shotgun victim Darryl Mackbee, Pastor Glenn E. Lassiter, Hunter's younger brother Jason (who works for the City of Long Beach), Sandy Samples (the one-time Westside gangbanger who witnessed Hunter's prison confrontation with Big John Cole), Lynwood "Speedy" Young, and Hussein Ayache, owner of the Pee & Gee Fish Market.

I became directly acquainted with Hunter's two surviving brothers, Jason and Robert; the story of the death of Hunter's older brother Eldridge is part of the book. I came to know three of Hunter's sisters—Desiree, Fabiola, Delreece—mostly through my interviews of Hunter, although I had several very pleasant chance-encounters with these women who shared Hunter's remarkable life story. Hunter's fourth and youngest sister, Nicole—whom I have not met—was adopted into the Hunter family shortly after Hunter's mother moved from New Orleans to Long Beach with her other seven children.

We chose not to interrupt the daily routine of Hunter's mother with any attempt to interview her, since Hunter's accounts of her life-struggles seemed sufficiently accurate and compelling. Finally, had he even survived the summer of 2008, we mostly likely would not have interviewed Hunter's father, since throughout Hunter's life, as the book describes, there was much stress in the relationship between Hunter and his father.

I have met all five of Hunter's children, four of whom are now adults. A main theme in the book is Hunter's intense efforts to relate carefully and lovingly to his children, in light of his own difficult relationship with his father and the nearly overwhelming circumstances of Hunter's life. These efforts, it appears to me, have had much to do with the fineness of these five children. Although Hunter's children are not the focus of any of the book's stories, all the children enter the stories indirectly through Hunter's account of parenting. Hunter's twin daughters, who are now young women, and his oldest son are mentioned openly in several of Hunter's stories, since those particular stories cannot otherwise be told.

I believe that Hunter's intelligence and rich life-experiences have made him an expert user of language. Hunter grew up in the South, ran with the West Coast gangs, and now has ten years of experience preaching to unusual and difficult audiences (mostly prison inmates). Accordingly, Hunter's language—which constitutes the core of this book—is a marvelous mixture of metaphors, slang, preaching, street language, King James English, story-telling, idioms and remembered-dialogue—all rooted in some wonderful way in Black Southern culture, the urban gang scene and Hunter's powerful mind. In the book, Hunter discusses Biblically-based stories and ideas that are familiar to most Christians—such as Jonah's unforgiveness, King David's transgressions and the love themes of 1 Corinthians 13—but does so with language that conveys new energy and insight. I find his use of language to be amazing and fun, especially when Hunter becomes emphatic in his speech or is particularly inspired by something he is saying. I have done my best to present Hunter's language in the book—not exactly as he spoke it, but pretty much so. It was my goal in editing the material to truly bring Hunter and his message to our readers.

We do not offer this book as strict Christian doctrine. The real power of the book comes from Hunter's account of the experiences that caused his relationship with God to grow. And those experiences, I believe, shape the way in which Hunter expresses his faith. Hunter's faith-experiences, rather than particular expressions of doctrine, form the core of this book.

Each chapter contains references to help the reader understand Hunter's topic; these are usually pieces of scripture from the New International Version of the Bible. My own interjections into Hunter's words, which I have tried to minimize, are given in square brackets (except that I myself have contributed one part of Chapter 5). Each chapter ends with added material— a "Study Guide"—to assist those readers who might choose to use the book as a devotional device or as a tool for group study.

The phases of Hunter's life roughly follow the decades (see *Chart: The Life of August Hunter, by Decade*, page 4). As described in Chapter 1, the 1960s were his childhood in New Orleans. Chapter 2 is set in the 1970s when Hunter grew in status as a "youngster" in the Long Beach gangs. The 1980s, chronicled in Chapter 3, were Hunter's years of prison (three separate terms, each about two years) and peak power in the Long Beach gangs. Chapters 4 and 5, set in the 1990s, describe Hunter's time in Long Beach, New Orleans and Portland, when the stress of Hunter's gangster lifestyle became too much and dramatic change began in Hunter's life. Chapters 6 and 7 describe the 2000s, when Hunter grew into his faith and began to build his new life as a San Diego pastor.

I have been profoundly encouraged and edified in my personal faith by the task of assembling this book. Hunter has convinced me all the more that God works deeply and deliberately through the experiences of our everyday lives and the people who surround us.

Dean A. Schiffman

Chart: The Life of August Hunter, by Decade

1960s   ❖ Childhood in New Orleans

1970s   ❖ Teenage years in the gangs, Long Beach, California

1980s   ❖ Prison term #1
            ❖ Rise to power in the adult Long Beach gangs
            ❖ Prison term #2
            ❖ New Orleans visit #1 (baptism)
            ❖ Return to Long Beach gangs
            ❖ Prison term #3 (parole violation)
            ❖ Return to Long Beach

1990s   ❖ New Orleans visit #2 (3 years)
            ❖ Brief return to Long Beach gangs
            ❖ Move to Portland
            ❖ Final break with the gangs
            ❖ Commitment to Chester's church

2000s   ❖ New job in San Diego
            ❖ Beginning of prison ministry
            ❖ The murder of Tracy Brown
            ❖ Mature prison ministry
            ❖ Marriage to Becky

Chapter 1 – Hard Start in the Big Easy

When my dad met my mom

Last Mother's Day I took my mom out to this Chinese buffet place that I know in Long Beach. We were sitting at a table and my mom was talking to my fiancée Becky. I was eating, but I was listening. And I was looking at my mom as she was talking with Becky about the things my dad did when they were still married, and that was bringing memories back to me. Back then I wanted to kill my dad.

My dad grew up in Mississippi. You have to understand my dad and his brothers and sisters and their mom and dad. To me, they were hillbillies. Those would be fightin' words if anyone else called them that. But I say they were hillbillies. They lived in the hills way out in the woods and they were pretty much cut off from civilization. Everything they did was like a farm person, not like a city person. Their next neighbor was twenty-five miles down the road.

My mom grew up in New Orleans and had seven sisters. No brothers.

When he was a young single man, my dad left Mississippi and made a trip to New Orleans, because he had some family there. He met my mom there and he hit her on the head with something and kidnapped her and took her back to their place in Mississippi. I had told Becky that story and she couldn't believe it; but then my mom shared it with her at the Chinese buffet place. "Yes. He hit me on the head, knocked me out and took me to Mississippi. His mother had me there for a week or two."

That must have happened around 1956 or 1957, because my older brother Eldridge was born in 1959 and I was born in 1960. Last July, when I went down to Mississippi for my dad's funeral, I saw how we had to drive deep, deep, deep—riding for a long time—to get to where they lived back then. My mom told me that after my dad hit her on the head, she woke up in a car way out there where they lived. My dad left her there with his mother and drove off. My dad's mother started crying because she knew what my dad did was wrong. When they got tired of her crying, one of my dad's brothers drove my mom back to New Orleans.

My dad hit my mom on the head with *something*. I always thought it was a bottle, but my sister says it was a club. When I was little, my dad worked on the waterfront and he always carried this pipe-thing that was a foot long. It was made of lead—real heavy—with leather over it that came to a loop at the end that you could put your hand through. He always kept that thing with him. I would think, *Wow! What does he do with this?* So maybe that's what he used to knock out my mom.

I don't know what my dad's mentality was back then. His intention was to keep my mom in Mississippi. But they finally ended up together in New Orleans, and my mom had seven kids by him—four boys and three girls. I can never sit down with my mom to find out exactly what happened. She shares little bits, but then she gets emotional about it.

So at the Chinese buffet place, after listening to my mom share those things with Becky, I had to get up and go get myself another plate of food, hoping that conversation would be done when I got back to the table. I wouldn't tell my mom to stop, because that was their conversation and my mom was having a good time. But when I came back to the table, they were still talking and my mom was bringing up more stuff that happened. It was just crazy, man.

Dad drove us to church

L ast week Becky and I were at my younger brother Robert's house. In his living room, above his fireplace, I saw some pictures of me and Robert when we were little boys, all dressed up.

I told Becky, "Hand me that picture." She handed me the picture and I asked her, "Do you know who this is?"

"No."

"That's me when I was little."

She said, "Is that you?" because I was real light-skinned back then.

That picture reminded me that when we were little boys, my dad would make us put on little suits, and then he would take all us kids to church. My dad was always big on church. He drove us to church every Sunday. He would put all seven of us kids into this little car that he owned and drive us to church; my mom never would go with us. He would drive us to my cousin's church, because my cousin was the pastor of the family.

On the way to church, my dad would wear his gun on his left side, under his suit coat. And he would roll up the windows of that car real tight and smoke marijuana all the way driving to church. When we finally got inside the church, all seven of us kids would sit down on the same pew and then fall asleep—knocked out! We would wonder, *Why is it that every time dad brings us to church, we fall asleep?*

Driving to church we could smell that stuff, but we just thought there was dead grass burning somewhere. When I got a little older, I found out that my dad kept a whole bunch of that dead grass in one of the drawers in his bedroom, and my friends started asking me for it.

Kindergarten robbery

W hen I started elementary school, my family was living in the housing projects in New Orleans. We were living in this one particular building, in an apartment unit on the second floor. Each unit up there had a little porch that you could step out on.

Each day, the schools would bus us from the projects to across town, and then bus us back again. When we got home from school each day, my parents would step out on that porch and watch the yellow school bus drop us off right there in front of our building. They would watch together from that porch.

I remember one day when I was in Kindergarten, I am getting off the yellow school bus and I am just behind this other boy. Then I reach one arm around that boy's neck and slip my other hand inside his pocket. My mom and dad saw that, and I got the whippin' of my life! As I got older, my dad would always tell me, "I knew right then I was gonna have problems with you. I seen a whole lotta me in you."

My dad knew where I was headed. My mom would cover for me and make excuses for me. But my dad saw that I was headed in the wrong direction. He and my mom would argue over that.

Chocolaty richness

Let the word of Christ dwell in you richly as you teach and admonish one another with all wisdom.

Colossians 3

It's so rich and thick and choco-lick, but you can't drink it slow if it's Quik!

Nesquik Bunny

It says, "Let the word of Christ dwell in you richly." Every time I read that passage, I think back to when I was a kid and I would watch cartoons on Saturday morning. I would love for this one commercial to come on the TV. It was a Nestlé commercial that had a rabbit who sang a little song, "It's so rich and thick and chocolaty, you can't get enough,...," or something like that. I loved that commercial.

So now, every time I read this passage from Colossians, it makes me think of that Nestlé commercial and letting the word of Christ dwell in us richly, like thick chocolate. We need to let the word of Christ be "so rich and thick and chocolaty" inside of us. Amen? I love this passage.

Our dog Brownie

In the book of 2 Samuel, King David took Uriah's wife Bathsheba for his own. Then David had Uriah killed. When that happened, the prophet Nathan told David a story, because David was so full of pride and so hung up on himself as king.

Nathan told King David about a poor man who only had one little ewe lamb, but the poor man loved that little ewe lamb. That little ewe lamb ate at the poor man's table with his children. That little ewe lamb was part of his family. But then a rich man took the little ewe lamb away from the poor man and slaughtered it, to feed his guest. After listening to the story, David got angry about what the rich man had done and yelled, "Who is that man?" Nathan said, "That man is you."

I can relate to that story because I remember when we were living in the projects, we found a little puppy. We named him Brownie. He was born with about an inch of tail and he was a mix of all kind of dog; he was one of them ol' ghetto dogs. We didn't know what kind of dog Brownie was, but he was *our* dog. We gave him our last name, so he became Brownie Hunter.

Brownie would have us laughin'—our family would drive off in our car and we would look back and see Brownie running after us behind the car. Wherever we went, Brownie would follow us across town, running after that car. Brownie loved being with us. We would kill anyone who tried to take Brownie away from us.

The beatings

My dad would beat me. You know, if you whoop a child, it's the *way* you do it that matters. I know I was a bad kid. But I didn't deserve what he did to me.

My dad would always find a wire or cord—like an extension cord—and whip me with that. He would punch me too. He would really do it to me, you know?

One night when I was in third or fourth grade, my dad came home drunk and couldn't find his gun. He thought me and my brothers stole it. He beat us down and put us out of the house. We stayed out all night, sleeping on the porch. My mom couldn't say anything or else he'd beat her down too.

My dad would talk crazy to me before he beat me. He would say real slow, "I- want- you- to- take- off- all- your- clothes." I would think, *Wow, I'm really gonna get it.* He would take that extension cord and he didn't care where that thing would hit me. He would rear back and then swing that thing at me, and it might catch me in the back of the head and wrap around so that I would get a welt across my face—that didn't matter to him; that didn't make him no different. I would think, *This dude is trying to kill me!* And you know how it hurts when you're crying and you're trying to block that extension cord so that it won't hit you in the face and then you accidentally touch him while you're doing that—he would say, "Aw! Now you're tryin' to hit me!" and he would pour even more on you.

That extension cord would tear my back all up. I would go to school—I remember the third grade—and my shirt would stick to my back because my dad had beat me. I couldn't even take my shirt off when I got home. I had to wet it down first, because it would be stuck to me—actually stuck to my back. And if I tried to just take it off, the scab on my back would peel right off with my shirt. After I got my shirt off, I would get my sisters to grease me down, because my back was so,...

It was something my dad had against me. My dad would sometimes beat my brothers, but he *always* beat *me*. My mom would ask him, "Why do you always beat *him*?" I couldn't breath without getting a whipping.

I cooled off

Fathers, do not embitter your children, or they will become discouraged.

Colossians 3

When I was growing up, I wanted to kill my dad. I always wanted to kill my dad because I thought he wasn't giving me a fair shake and he didn't like me. There'd be days when I would be so mad—because he had whooped me that day—that I wanted to shoot my dad when he came home. My dad would leave the house; then I would find his gun and I would wait for him.

One day I was feeling that I really *could* shoot my dad. Then right before he got home, I put the gun away. You know—I cooled off.

Living in boxes

You can read in the book of 1 Kings, the second chapter, where King David is dying, and he shares all his bitterness with his son Solomon, bitterness that David had not dealt with. David told Solomon, "Now you yourself know what Joab son of Zeruiah did to me. Do not let his gray head go down to the grave in peace." David also said, "And remember, you have with you Shimei son of Gera, the Benjamite from Bahurim, who called down bitter curses on me. Bring his gray head down to the grave in blood."

People say Solomon's trouble as king started when he was dealing with his seven-hundred wives, living in a palace. But no. Solomon's troubles started when his father David laid all that bitterness on Solomon. Bitterness like that will cause you to do things that are harmful. That's why Jesus said in Mark 11, "And when you stand praying, if you hold anything against anyone, forgive him, so that your Father in heaven may forgive you your sins." Let that bitterness go.

That helps me love my dad with a genuine love. I remember one time when my dad beat me so bad that I ran away from home. I was eight years old. There was a furniture store down the block from our house. I went behind that furniture store and I found some big boxes. I lived back there in those boxes for five days. It was cold. Man, I was *sleeping* in those boxes.

Something finally made me come out of those boxes and go home. I had to face another whippin'. But I look back and think, *God saved me through all that.* So I forgive and I let go of my own bitterness, and that helps me to be able to love.

Tiger, Rusty and Weasel

When I was about eight years old, I had a friend named Tiger. He lived downstairs from us in the projects. Tiger's family loved me, because they knew what my dad was doing to me, and Tiger's dad didn't like it.

I think back—Tiger was Hispanic! I didn't know he was Hispanic that whole time, because he was my friend. You know what I'm saying? I didn't consider that he was a different color than me.

I *never* had a friend like Tiger. I loved Tiger because he was adventurous. We'd go out and look for trouble. I *knew* we were gonna have some fun—we were gonna go climb over somebody's fence and dig in their peach tree, or climb over somebody's fence and dig in their apple tree, or we were gonna hop a train and beat up the hobos and throw them off the train. We just *did* stuff, you know? We were some bad kids!

I had another friend named Rusty, a little freckle-faced White kid. He would hang out with me and Tiger, to go get in trouble. Whenever we found trouble, Rusty would just stand there; he wouldn't put his hand to the plow, you know? But Rusty would be right there coaching us on—"Let's do it! Let's do it!" And when we got caught, Rusty would be just as guilty, because he was there with us.

Rusty was fun because he got whatever he wanted from his parents. So we could go over to Rusty's house and hang out and play games and do whatever we wanted, because his mom was gone. Rusty's dad stayed home to watch us, but—heck—we would watch *him*. He would make us laugh. But any drunk will make you laugh.

We had another friend named Weasel. I think he was Hispanic too. Weasel could steal without showing anything on his face; I could never do that. One day at Weasel's house we were playing with his dad's .410 shotgun. We dropped it and it went off. *BLOOM!* Weasel got worried. He said, "We better put this away, so my dad don't find out." I said, "What about that hole in the ceiling?" Somehow we never heard more about that.

Every time I got together with Tiger, Rusty and Weasel, I got a whoopin'—because we went out and we got in trouble and we ended up in juvenile hall or the police would bring us home. Our families tried to keep us apart, but we were friends; they were my family. Whenever I got mad at home, I would just tell myself, *I'll go find Tiger.*

Looking back, when I was running with Tiger and Rusty and Weasel, that was me reaching out for love from a male perspective. That's what I was doing. I knew I would get a whoopin', but I looked forward to hanging out with those guys—just doing stuff—because it was fun. It happened to me again later, when me and my mom moved to Long Beach and I got introduced to the gangs; I wasn't getting love from a male perspective because my dad was not there. So I embraced the gangs.

My first twenty-dollar bill

I remember one Christmas—I will never forget it. My dad gave all us kids twenty dollars apiece. That was huge back then—in 1968 or 1969.

Then I got in trouble with Tiger. I think I shot a girl in the eye with a slingshot, or something. Her parents called the police. My dad beat me like I had stole the government's mule.

The next day was Christmas and my dad took my twenty-dollar bill away from me. My sisters and brothers all still had their twenty-dollar bills. But he took mine away. That hurt me so bad. I thought he would take it away and then give it back to me later. But he never gave it back to me. I thought, *That's all I had for Christmas.*

As kids you look for special things to happen. On Halloween, we would go out trick-or-treating. As a kid, I identified Easter with rabbits and chocolate eggs, and we looked forward to that. Even today, I am careful not to deprive my kids of that. So Christmas was a time when we expected special gifts and prizes. That Christmas all we got was a twenty-dollar bill. That meant so much to me. But my dad took it away.

There was other stuff like that that happened. Even back then I felt, *When I have kids, they will know that they have a daddy.* Today I have a relationship with my kids. I would never rob them.

Do unto others

My dad did *nothin'* for us when we were little. As a matter of fact, he did things to *hurt* us. He would do for other people and not do for us, like the time he was staying with us and we needed a refrigerator but he bought the lady next door a refrigerator.

In the fourth grade, I wanted to play in the band. I wanted to blow a saxophone. I had that desire, you know? So I shared that with my mom and dad. But there was a friend of my dad's that had a kid that wanted to play music, and my dad went out and bought *that* kid a saxophone—maybe it was a clarinet he bought, I'm not sure. But that ripped me up. That devastated me. Playing saxophone was my desire, and it never happened. I lost interest when my dad bought that kid a saxophone. I could have been a jazz musician, because I was interested in that—deeply. But my dad took that away from me.

Back then my mom struggled from job to job. My dad lived in the house and he was making big money, but he would give my mom only $100 a month for us. He was so cold.

My dad would say bad things about my mom and us to other people, right in front of us! He cared for other people more than us, and that hurt. It hurt to see my dad cater to other people.

Even after I was an adult, whenever my dad got some money, he would call me just to tell me that he was going to do this or that for some other person. I'd say to him, "That's good. Praise the Lord," and then he'd tell me something else he was going to do for them. That made me think, *Wow, man! Do you ever stop?* There were people at my dad's funeral that my dad had helped that way. All my kinfolks wanted to jump 'em. But I told them, "Naw. Let 'em go."

With my dad, it was always hurt, it was always somethin' derogatory, it was always things said that were *designed* to really hurt you. And it was always beatings and whippings and punishment—and nothin', nothin', nothin' representin' love. He'd tell us, "Aw, I love you all. You're my daughter. You're my son. You've got to have a relationship with God." But in actions, he never showed nothin' from love. Even when my older brother died, he came out to California and helped do the funeral. He did the funeral, but he didn't show my brother no love. And someone who was looking in from the outside would never have been able to tell—by the way we operated, by the way we communicated, by the things that we did—that we were father and son. You wouldn't have ever thought that.

Dope in the drawer

Growing up in the projects, I had time on my hands. I could do whatever I wanted. The older guys would let me hang out with them. I was eight or nine, and these guys were eighteen, nineteen, twenty years old. They were gangsters. I was even drinking with them; they thought it was so funny to have a kid out there drinking with them.

My dad kept a drawer full of marijuana. He kept a pound at a time. Those older guys knew that my dad kept marijuana and they were always asking me to get them some. I would take a little brown paper bag and open my dad's drawer and put in some of that stuff. Those guys would ask me for that every day, and I would always go get them some.

It was crazy in the projects. It was nothing for us to wake up in the morning, get ready for school, leave our unit on the second floor and find someone in the hallway on the first floor, dead from some activity the night before. Police—all day, every day. Constant fighting and shooting. I grew up in all of that. So I thought it was something huge for those older guys to ask me to assist them in stealing marijuana from my dad. I felt they were embracing me. I felt like I was part of their gang. They were respecting me and recognizing me. The younger guys my own age would ask me, "Why do those guys like you more than us?" That meant a lot to me.

From brother Jason

[Contribution from Hunter's youngest brother, Jason]

Our dad came from old-fashioned ways. His way was, *This is how it's done, no matter if it's crushing you.* August would try to work with my dad, but my dad could be real cruel—my mother is the giving one. When my dad got into those areas of unfairness, that's where my dad and August would part. August would challenge him.

Ending in New Orleans

I look back on the streets of New Orleans. I liked to run with the older guys there. I wanted to be part of whatever they were doing. I didn't care what it would cost me or where it would land me. That made no difference to me, as long as I could be part of that.

I just started living the life of a criminal, way back then. I wasn't looking at it as being a criminal. I was just having fun. I was always away from my family. They wouldn't see me all day, every day.

By the time I was ten or eleven years old, my dad was just a mess—he stayed drunk, stayed smokin' that marijuana, carried a gun. No one dealt with him because he was crazy—not even his own family, because they were scared to death of him.

And it was just getting worse and worse. So my mom and dad split up. My mom's sisters and her mother had moved out to California. So that's where we went—Long Beach. We were the last of the family—meaning us and all my mother's sisters—to leave New Orleans.

That's when my life took a total turn. I had grown up in the gangs down in New Orleans. So when I got to Long Beach, I found out that it was *infested* with gangs. I told myself, *Wow! This is my type of stuff right here!*

Chapter 1 Study Guide

When my dad met my mom

Every person's life is, more or less, a mixture of pain and productivity. God knows this. Jesus experienced it. As God works with us to enrich our lives, He accounts for the pain of past hurts. And He can heal those hurts if we let Him. If life is a mixture of pain and productivity, how do you experience each of those in your daily life? Is there pain in your life that you are trying to ignore?

Dad drove us to church

We practice our faith in an imperfect world. We go to church, but we live daily in a world full of hypocrisy, danger and cynicism. Children observe all this, and we cannot hide it all from them. But we can, through our own lives, demonstrate authentic faith-based living. If, on the other hand, we are part of the hypocrisy, the impact on a child's faith and development can be devastating. Were you ever discouraged in your faith by someone of influence? Do you have trouble integrating your faith with your daily living?

Kindergarten robbery

If we see a child headed in a wrong direction, we need to discover what is wrong in that child's life. Childish attempts at theft, for example, are often the result the child's need for intimacy, since the theft provides a temporary feeling of connection with the stolen object. If both parents are available to work with a misguided child, they need to be united in their efforts. That will last the child a lifetime. Do you have or know a troubled child whose bad behavior is rooted in deeper causes?

Chocolaty richness

What do children "taste" when they meet adult Christians? Is it joy, courage, vitality? Or is it blandness? Jesus called us to be salt, adding flavor to life. If children taste something in us, they too will be drawn to him, instead of to drugs, money and prestige. Does God's word dwell in you richly? Are you salty in life, or have you lost your saltiness?

Our dog Brownie

Pets are an example of the simple goodness of life. They evoke in us the love and closeness that we all yearn to experience more regularly. They brighten our lives even in the worst of circumstances. That's why Nathan's story was so effective in humbling King David.

Like King David, we can get confused and distracted by the empty things of life—money, career, power—and move away from its simple joys. What earthly attractions are hardest for you to resist? Remember the story of Brownie, and compare it to "My dog Noodles," found later in the book.

Page 19

The beatings

In dysfunctional families, everyone is simply trying to survive, especially the children. One way to survive is to adopt a particular role in the family—the responsible one, the adjuster, the comic, or the scapegoat. It is the scapegoat who takes on the illness of the family.

Parents who are out of control are not managing their feelings. Instead of seeing anger as a signal that something is wrong internally, they misdirect the anger outward, generally toward the scapegoat or the most sensitive child who will take it. That damages a young life, destroys a child-parent relationship, and keeps the abusive parent ignorant of what is actually wrong. What feelings did one of your parents have trouble managing? Have you learned a better way to manage those same feelings?

I cooled off

Justice is not just a legal concept. It is basic to daily life and our personal relationships. The Bible tells us that justice is central to God's character. If someone has wronged us and there has been no resolution—no justice—we suffer hurt and emotional pain. And it takes energy to push that pain away each day. Among your family and friends, are you a source of justice or injustice? Are you yourself suffering from a longstanding injustice?

Living in boxes

Children and teenagers who leave home face insurmountable circumstances, and may barely get a chance to forgive those who harm them. But God is there for them, through us and others, although the process of forgiveness and healing may take a lifetime. Have you ever felt like running away from your family, your job, your marriage? Are there opportunities in your life to forgive people who have hurt you?

Tiger, Rusty and Weasel

Many successful individuals have been raised by a single mom doing an excellent job. But a caring dad, in most cases, would have made a difference. Without a role model, boys who are looking to become grown men are forced to make it up out of nowhere. Having a roadmap helps. Girls get much of their self-esteem from their fathers. If a girl's father tells her she is worthwhile, intelligent, special, pretty, she will have an added dose of confidence and will search out a partner who appreciates her. Girls can still otherwise be successful, but picking a healthy partner may not go as smoothly. Should your father have invested more in you? How would things have been different? If you are a father, can you improve in this area?

My first twenty-dollar bill

Parents provide necessities to their children, such as food, clothing and shelter. But children should get something more from their parents. Children need to be given hope, joy, imagination, inspiration and courage. Children can become debilitated when these things are not provided. If you are a parent, do you provide inspiration to your children, or just the necessities? How was your life improved or diminished by a parent who did or did not inspire you?

Do unto others

Some parents deliberately discourage their children. They discourage children by taking away precious rights—the right to feel important, the right to belong, the right to enjoy (to learn about the wonder of God's world) and the right to feel. God intends to use families to deploy those rights to children, not to extinguish them. Did your parents approach their parenting job constructively or negatively? What difference did that make?

Dope in the drawer

To gain approval, we sometimes put ourselves together with people who take advantage of us. Having a relationship, even a bad one, seems better than going it alone. Having a bad thing to fill a void sometimes seems better than living with the void. But when you value yourself and feel connected to God, you have a way of surviving loneliness. Where do you let others take advantage of you? At work? In relationships? With family? What have you compromised in order to be accepted?

Ending in New Orleans

So much of what happens to us in life is rooted in our childhood and the influence of our parents. We should not underestimate the power of this. As we face new challenges in our lives—as Hunter did when he moved to Long Beach—the lessons of our childhood either play out more fully, or a process of change begins, depending on how we react. Do you feel that the basic patterns of your childhood have had influence in your life? How have you altered these patterns?

Chapter 2 – Long Beach - "Infested" With Gangs

New kid in the neighborhood

My life took a total turn when my parents split up and I moved to California with my mom. I was eleven years old. I found out that Long Beach was *infested* with gangs. There was a gang for older guys called the 21st Street Black Lords. There was another gang called the Artistics; those guys were my age. That's where I first met Glenn Lassiter, when we were in the Artistics together. When we got older, Glenn became a pastor.

I worked my way into the Long Beach gangs using my fists. That was because back in New Orleans, I did some boxing. I would hang out at the Boy's Club where they had boxing equipment and they had guys there who were trained to box. It was nothing serious, but I was good. They called me a "knock-out artist."

So when I was new in Long Beach, I would battle with the guys in the Artistics every day. They called me "that ol' country boy," and they hated me because I could *fight!* I would catch each one of them by themselves and punch 'em out. The older gangsters were hearing about it. They'd ask, "Who's this country boy that's been moppin' up all the youngsters in the Artistics?" They all wanted to meet me. So I started running with the older guys again, and the Artistics respected that.

I was about thirteen or fourteen years old when I started getting serious in the gangs. It was the Artistics first, then the Black Lords, and then the Rollin' 20's Crips. My cousin Tony had a lot to do with starting the Rollin'

20's there. He was "Big Cat" and I was "Big Dog." He's in the federal penitentiary right now.

Because I was good with my fists, I moved up fast in the Long Beach gangs; I didn't go in much for gun play. If I had to do somethin' to a guy, I'd just lay hands on him.

Grandpa August

"Come, follow me," Jesus said, "and I will make you fishers of men."

Mark 1

My mom's dad was named August too—Grandpa August. He had eight daughters, and no boys. I think they were all embarrassed by him, because he was a straight alcoholic. But I loved Grandpa August. When he died, it tore me up.

Even before Grandpa August—*his* dad was also named August. So to keep that name going—after my older brother was named Eldridge, after my dad—my parents gave *me* that name. Grandpa August once told me, "When I heard they was gonna name you after me, I decided I was gonna *kill* ya! Yep! *Drown* ya! I was already drawin' the bathwater. Who wants a name like *that?*"

Grandpa August would always say to his grandsons, "You ain't nothin' but a hermaphrodite! That's right—a little hermaphrodite!" When I got older I looked that word up in the dictionary and I said, "Grandpa, *that's* what you were calling us?"

Whenever you were with him, Grandpa August was always serious at the start. But when you got that first beer in him, he was the life of the party. Grandma couldn't handle him. He would start calling her "Margaret," and whoever he was talking to, "you MF!" He couldn't handle hard liquor, but it seemed like beer was even worse for him.

Grandpa August loved to go fishing down in Long Beach Harbor, by the Queen Mary. He would say to the boys, "I'm goin' fishin'. Wanna go?"

but not to the girls. When we went fishing with Grandpa, we always had another adult along with us—because of how he got after that first beer—but we loved to hear Grandpa talk. All I knew about fishing before then was from New Orleans down by the waterfront where the ships would tie up and my brother Eldridge would bait a trotline with all sorts of things—little shrimps, pieces of bread, old chunks of fish—and tie it to a bollard; then we would run off somewhere else and come back and there would be a string of serious catfish on that trotline—big catfish with big ol' heads. But from that type of fishing, I never learned about just sitting and talking. I learned that from Grandpa August.

We would sit and catch perch and flounder, and then me and the other kids would go exploring around by the Queen Mary. When we were done for the day, Grandpa would clean our fish right there and we would take them home to fry up. It was fun. We always knew we would have fun fishing with Grandpa August. He was a good fisherman.

About that time—I was thirteen or fourteen years old—I started smoking marijuana with my friend Harvey. That stuff, man! After one or two puffs, we started gigglin' so hard our stomach muscles would seize up. Then Harvey would say, "Let's go talk to your Grandpa!" and I'd say, "You just wanna laugh at my Grandpa," because Grandpa would always wake up from being drunk and his hair would be flying all over and he would talk crazy—but he was trying to be serious—and we would laugh at that.

With Grandpa August, it was one beer—then another and another and another. But I loved him, man.

My adopted sister

When we first moved to Long Beach, there was this one family that lived by us. One of the girls in that family had a baby girl, but she couldn't take care of that baby, so my mom did. My mom ended up adopting that baby. She became my youngest sister, Nicole, who is incarcerated now.

Nicole has had problems. She got in with this group of girls and they hurt her. One day they called our house and said, "Come get your sister. She's around the corner, bleedin'." I thought that would scare Nicole back into doing what's right. But it didn't.

Nicole had four children. My oldest sister Desiree adopted each one of them, and they are doing good. I have it in my heart to be able to win Nicole over for Christ. But she is still never where I am able to deal with her.

Meeting gangsters

The neighborhood would have house parties. That's how I met the gangsters. There would be pretty girls there—my sisters, cousins, and their friends. They were pretty girls, and that would bring the gangsters around.

Doing tricks

Then the LORD God said to the woman, "What is this you have done?" The woman said, "The serpent deceived me, and I ate."

Genesis 4

When I was a teenager, me and my little homeboys were hustlers. We would hang around this apartment complex owned by one of the pimps we knew, but we had to hide. All the tricks would come there to meet up with his girls. When the tricks pulled up in their car, they would get out their wallet and take out enough money for inside the place, then hide their wallet somewhere in the car—in the glove compartment or under the front seat—and go inside. That's when we would break into their car and steal their wallet and whatnot. It was amazing that those guys would come to that place with a lot of money, maybe two or three thousand dollars in their wallet.

At that time I had two homeboys that were brothers; right now they are both doing life sentences in the penitentiary. They had a sister that was real beautiful, and I liked her. She could have been my girlfriend. But this one pimp, he overdosed her on heroin. Me and my homeboys were all mad because she was our age and those older guys made her hang out with them. She was young and these pimps were older. I hated it when they did that to her. It messed me up.

Then there was this pimp—he pimped his own daughter! Yeah, he was a trip. His daughter's name was ____, and he pimped her; she eventually got out of that and now she is walkin' with the Lord. At that time, we knew what the pimps were like. But I didn't know the depth of it.

So I grew up hating the pimps. I hated that they killed my homeboys' sister and I liked her. When we got older, we would go find the pimps that came through Long Beach and rob them. We would beat them too, just to hear them holler. They were soft guys. But they were hard on women.

Chicken George

There were three of us teenagers. The neighborhood called us, "The Three Stooges." There was me. Then there was my homeboy Trent who lived on the other side of Martin Luther King Park; Trent is in the federal penitentiary now. And then there was George, who lived next door to me; he was my best friend; we called him Chicken George.

Chicken George's mother was a good cook, but she was a *real* good gambler. Even when Chicken was a baby, she had a reputation as a gambler, a reputation for winning all the money all the time. It was a gift she had, and she passed that gift down to Chicken George. Chicken knew cards, dice, dominoes—you name it. He knew stuff that the big-time gamblers didn't know, and he was a kid.

Chicken George was a marksman when it came to money. All us guys would get together to have fun and maybe smoke some PCP. But as soon as there was money there, Chicken George would just snap out of it and get right to that money. We called him Chicken because when he showed up, he would just *peck* at your money until he had it all. And he could count money—big time. He was good at math. It was that gift his mom gave him.

There was this apartment building across the street from where we lived, on Salt Lake Street. It had three stoops out in front that were sort of spread out. We would have a big dice game goin' on each stoop—every day, all day. Everybody would come to gamble there. Chicken and I would operate the gambling all day long, and each day we would end up winning all the money. That started to give us a problem, because the people who would come to gamble there would say to me, "Why does Chicken keep winnin' all the money?"

We would go into the gambling shacks—where the roughest, most dangerous people would be—and get the money out of those places. I'd say, "Chicken, I don't know how you do it, but you always do it!" Everybody in the neighborhood that had anything to do with money, me and Chicken would beat them out of every dime.

But we had to work as a team. Chicken would get himself into some dice game and would be winning all the money, and I would walk up out of nowhere and see the dice game and Chicken in the middle of it, and Chicken would look up and he would have this expression on his face like, *Man, I sure am glad to see you!* When that happened, I would get Chicken out of there and then Chicken would split the money with me and Trent, sometimes thousands of dollars. So a lot of times Chicken would gamble and get himself into a dangerous situation, but Trent and I would fight his battles. People knew that if you did something to Chicken, August and Trent wouldn't let you get away with it. Chicken would do all the gambling, and if there was an argument, I would step up. Or I could get physical; I could do that. My job was to make sure that Chicken didn't get hurt and that we got out of there with all the money.

We had this bully in the neighborhood named John Cole. He was an older guy, a big dude—like Magilla Gorilla! He had twenty-four inch arms and weighed three hundred pounds.

I knew John Cole at that time—when Chicken and Trent and I were youngsters—but years later, John Cole and I would be in the penitentiary together. Even there, the whole prison was afraid of John. The guards hated him. We played dominoes in prison, and if John's partner played the wrong domino, John might swing across the table and knock him out and make some other inmate take his place. One time John stole a piece of pipe from the prison weight pile and hid it in his bunk in the dormitory. A while later, John and I were playing dominoes in the dormitory and the janitor—this White inmate—came in to mop up. He said, "You guys need to take your game outside and let me mop up." John said, "Okay. Just hold on," and John went off and got that pipe and came back and beat that janitor half to death. There was blood everywhere. John was just that vicious.

But before that, back in the neighborhood, John had a reputation for beating people up and for shooting people in the back. He liked to drink gin straight from the bottle. He would drink so much of that stuff that he would sweat and you could smell that gin comin' right out of him. He would always be full of gin and talkin' crazy.

But Chicken George had those gambling skills. One morning John Cole brought six or seven thousand dollars to Martin Luther King Park, and we started gambling and Chicken started winning John's money. Every time Chicken would win some of John's money he would just slide it over to me and I would hold that money, because we knew that John would try to grab Chicken and take all that money back.

Finally Chicken worked John down to about thirty dollars, and John wouldn't let Chicken leave. John said, "No! You're stayin' here," and he told one of his boys, "Go get me more money!"

When it started getting dark, I got worried. I said, "Chicken, we need to leave."

"No, August. He might shoot me."

I said, "Chicken, you need to just take off runnin'. He ain't never gonna just *let* you leave."

"Man, you're right! He *ain't* gonna just let me leave!"

Then John told Chicken, "You better not leave here with my money!"

I told John, "It ain't your money no more. Chicken won it!"

He said, "You stay out of this Dog! Let me deal with Chicken," because John knew how we worked together.

So I finally made Chicken just *run* out of there. I told him, "Just take off runnin'. Go man! Now!" and he took off running across the park and I yelled, "Go man! Go! Keep goin'!"

For a while, John was driving around the neighborhood looking for Chicken. He wanted to do something to Chicken. But we hid Chicken from him, because John was just an evil dude. Wherever he went, he left a trail of mess. Later, when John and I were in the penitentiary together, I ended up knocking him on his butt.

That's what me and Trent and Chicken did when we were young. That is how we got our money, because we weren't going out robbing people. Gambling meant that I had money to take care of my sisters and brothers. When Christmas time came—or any holiday—we always had money, because me and Chicken lived next door to each other. We got money from gambling—to take care of our family, to do things, to buy clothes and pay bills. You know what I'm saying? We were a team. That was one way we took care of ourselves in the neighborhood, growing up there. Chicken's mom is still around, cooking. But she gave Chicken those gambling skills.

Phencyclidine

> *Phencyclidine (PCP)--A dissociative drug formerly used as an anesthetic agent, exhibiting hallucinogenic and neurotoxic effects. Although the primary psychoactive effects of the drug last only hours, total elimination from the body is prolonged, typically extending over weeks.*
>
> *--Wikipedia*

If you could go back and look at my neighborhood in the 1970s, you would see people all over the place that were holding on to a fence or holding on to a tree or holding on to a wall, because if they don't hold on, they will fall down. We called them "soakin' wet," which meant they had smoked PCP. It was like they were on an island by themselves.

Back then, the Compton gangs were known for cooking up PCP. They would break into mortuaries to get the embalming fluid that was meant for the dead bodies, because that was a main ingredient for making PCP. Once they made that PCP, they would dip in a marijuana cigarette and make a Sherm stick. That was one of the most powerful, most requested drugs back then. They were making a lot of money off that stuff.

PCP was powerful. It could make you high for two or three days. Gangsters would smoke that stuff before they went on a killing spree; their mind would be gone. If the police caught you full of that stuff, they might just shoot you, because they knew people were breaking out of handcuffs and doing unreal stuff, like they had super-strength or something.

I had one homeboy who was a big ol' guy. If you boxed him, you wouldn't even last one round, so we called him One Round. One Round loved smoking PCP. One time we found him on 17th Street, right before it got dark. His car was in the middle of the street—engine running, doors open, headlights on—and One Round was just standing out in front of it with a Sherm stick in his hand. He was stuck. We tried to snap him out of it, but we couldn't. He was like a statue. Another time, One Round got full of PCP and started walking downtown, and downtown is a long ways off from our neighborhood. He just started walking downtown, real fast. I asked him later, "One Round, where were you walkin' to?" He said, "I don't know. I just kept walkin' and walkin', all the way downtown. Then I walked into the police station and up to the counter. I still had that Sherm stick in my hand and they took it away and put on the handcuffs. Then they locked me up." I said, "One Round, you walked yourself to jail?" He said, "I don't know why I did that." I laughed and told him, "Wow, man. We don't want nothin' like *that!*"

PCP takes away your mind. I am still acquainted with people that I smoked it with in the 70s. They are still living in the 70s, you know what I mean? They are still there. I thank God, because I still have a mind. I can remember my name. I thank Him for that.

My older brother Eldridge

> *Absalom ordered his men, "Listen! When Amnon is in high spirits from drinking wine and I say to you, 'Strike Amnon down,' then kill him."*
>
> *2 Samuel 13*

King David's son Absalom killed his brother Amnon for raping their sister Tamar. Then Absalom turned against his father David and took away his kingdom. See, David brought all that mess down on his family by his sin with Bathsheba. David found out that our sin not only affects us, it affects all those who are close around us. We have to be aware of what we get ourselves involved in.

I had an older brother who died from cirrhosis of the liver. He was named after my father, Eldridge. I always picked up real fast on things, but

Eldridge was slow. He wasn't real slow, but he was sort of slow. Knowing that he was slow, I loved my brother. I cared for him so much. We would fight all the time, him and me and my other brothers. But I would not allow anyone else to disrespect him.

Eldridge admired me, because all the gangsters hung out with me. He thought that was cool. He would mimic the stuff that I did. Me and the homeboys would hang out and drink and smoke weed, and my brother would do that too. But him being slow, he didn't realize that he was killing himself. He would drink every day and never eat. You couldn't tell him nothin', but at the same time, he didn't know nothin'. I tried to talk to him, but he would not listen. All I could do is sit back and watch my brother die. I look back on that and I think, *If only I could have got hold of my brother.*

God brought me to this story of David's family because I think I was responsible for bringing my brother to a bad situation—the situation of wanting to hang out and drink and do the stuff that I did. He liked what I did. He would mimic. It stemmed from me, you know?

I just thank God that it did not affect all the rest of my brothers and sisters. My older brother was the only other one that ended up in prison like I did. He wasn't even that type of guy, but he ended up going to prison following behind me.

Right before my brother died, I had him coming to church with me. Now he's not here.

I didn't know better

I grew up in the gang life. I didn't just jump into it. I thought it was normal. I thought this is what the world consisted of. I thought this was the way to take care of myself. I didn't know better.

When I was younger, I was always running with the big boys, proving myself. As I got older, I got noticed and talked about, especially when I had to put hands on older guys. Before you know it, I was already up for the position of leadership in the serious gangs, in the Rollin' 20's Crips.

Chapter 2 Study Guide

New kid in the neighborhood

God provides power in our lives, in appropriate ways and at appropriate times. But many of us fail to tap that power. Instead, we seek earthly power—money, prestige, intimidation. That type of power may move us up the corporate ladder, get us into the right social circle or put us at the top of a gang. But there is often no internal peace with earthly power. It requires constant watchfulness. Do you rely on earthly power instead of God's power? What would your days be like if you relied more on God's power?

Grandpa August

A parent's approval means the world to a child; a parent's disapproval can crush a child's wellbeing. Grandparents wield even more power in a child's life, especially those grandparents who have regular contact with their grandchildren. More important, Grandpa August was a beloved figure in the family, in spite of his flaws. His strengths—his ability to relate and his willingness to spend time with loved ones—were cherished by those around him. What powerful positive or negative messages did you receive as a child? What difference did they make?

Doing tricks

In the book of Genesis, the Bible tells us that human beings are valuable because they are made in God's image. When we look at human beings we should be awed at the wonder of God's greatest creation. Yet we routinely mistreat one another, even within our own family. Why is it we do not stand in awe of each other as God's creation? Instead, we inflict psychological and emotional pain on each other, even those of us who consider ourselves to be believers. What is in your heart that allows you to treat people with less than the utmost grace and respect? What happens in our country and in the world when we forget that people are God's greatest creation, made in His image?

Chicken George

God gives us the talents and skills that allow our community to function and flourish. Chicken George and August figured out their own system for pooling their gifts, to make life better for themselves. It is a funny twist on

God's plan, but it worked for them, resulting in love and respect between them. Are you aware of gifts or special abilities you have that you can share with others to enrich their lives? Do you under-utilize those gifts?

Phencyclidine

Generally, there is emotional pain behind any substance abuse. Alcohol or drugs becomes a cover for pain. But no amount of alcohol, PCP, marijuana—whatever—takes away emotional pain permanently. It is a temporary emotional anesthetic that leads to yet another problem. God has provided for healthy ways to deal with emotional pain—tears, His comfort, reading the Bible, friendship, the listening ear of someone who loves us, journaling, painting, helping others, and so on. What do you rely on to cover pain? What provisions are you failing to draw on to deal with your own pain?

My older brother Eldridge

We all have some influence, because of the people around us. Whether as family members, friends, coworkers, or neighbors, our lives come up against other lives. That influence can contribute positively through such attributes as kindness, generosity, integrity and support. Or it can contribute negatively in our being mean-spirited, spiteful, self-righteous, self-centered or inconsiderate. Opportunities to influence are precious. To miss them is tragically wasteful. What God-given gift do you use to enrich the lives of those around you? If you could redo some relationships in your life, who would that be with and what would you change?

I didn't know better

Children have been known to leave their homes at night and wander the neighborhood peering into other homes, to see whether those other homes are like their own. If you grow up not realizing that there are experiences different than your own, you may never break out of your own circumstances and strive for something better. What events in your life helped you to grow beyond your family? Who or what has God provided to help you with that?

Chapter 3 – The Penitentiary

Jailhouse justice

Be sure of this: The wicked will not go unpunished, but those who are righteous will go free.

Proverbs 11

When I was twenty years old I went on trial for burglary, together with an older guy that I was running around with. He was the one who got caught with the jewelry and the money, but he tried to make it look like I did everything. This was his third time going to the penitentiary and the District Attorney was looking to put him in there for a long time.

When I was in the jail waiting to go to trial, there were these other guys in there also, waiting. I already had a reputation for fighting and they respected me. They wanted to jump all over this guy who was on trial with me, because I was a youngster and he was older and he was trying to double-cross me. They told me, "Man, he's trying to give you that whole case. We won't let him!"

When the trial came, the DA told the jury, "This kid—August Hunter. I don't care if he gets a year. I don't care if he gets probation. I don't even care if he gets cut loose! I don't want August Hunter. I want *him!*" and he pointed to the other guy. It turned out, that guy got sentenced to eleven years in prison. I got sixteen months, and I actually *did* a little more than a year, from the end of 1980 to the start of 1982.

That guy I went to trial with is still locked up in prison. He got out a couple times after our case, but he got himself back in again. He is just straight institutionalized, and he is in his fifties now.

I'm gonna have to kill this guy!

Pride goes before destruction, a haughty spirit before a fall.

Proverbs 16

Yeah, I was there. It happened so fast. BAM! I was thinking—Damn, August just knocked down John Cole! Oh yeah, it's on now!

Sandy Samples

After my trial for burglary, I was sent to the penitentiary for the first time. When I got to the penitentiary, John Cole was already there. He was a bully from back in my neighborhood. He had twenty-four inch arms and weighed over three hundred pounds. Older guy. He had a reputation for shooting people in the back and beating people up. John knew me from the neighborhood, so he took me under his wing—me and a couple of other youngsters including my homeboy Sandy Samples from the Westside, who was seventeen.

We would all lift weights at the prison weight pile out in the yard. John Cole was pushing the most weight of all the inmates, bench pressing five hundred pounds. I weighed only one hundred and eighty pounds myself, but I was bench pressing three hundred.

John Cole had a habit that I never liked: He would practice punching on us youngsters. The other youngsters would accept it and just keep their mouth shut. But that punching was one thing I could not *stand!* John thought it was so funny, because he saw how angry I would get when he punched me. I'd tell him, "Stop playin' with me. I don't like it!" John had these other guys his own age out there in the prison yard who were his butt-kissers. So they had to laugh whenever John would punch on us.

There was this one day—I remember it like it was yesterday. Here I am in prison. I am already angry that day—even before I meet up with John Cole—because I missed breakfast. Sandy Samples is with me and we are heading for the weight pile, where John is.

I tell Sandy, "Man, I hope John don't put his hands on me, playin'. I'm not feelin' it today, bro'."

Sandy says, "August, we don't need to go over there today."

I say, "No. This is our time slot. We need to go over there."

Me and Sandy get over to the weight pile and, sure enough, John starts playing around, punching me and laughing.

I tell him, "John, I don't feel like this today."

John says, "Aw August, stop bein' a buster."

I say, "Don't put your hands on me, man."

John yells, "Are you threatenin' me youngster? You threatenin' me? Huh?" Now every inmate in the yard is watching us.

I say, "No. I'm not threatenin' you, man. But don't you put your hands on me today."

Then John punches me one more time on the chest and my reflexes kick in and—*BAM!*—I knock him hard on his jaw with my fist and John flies up in the air and comes down right on his butt. Oh my *God* I hit him hard!

Now you have to understand that the weight pile is a square area filled with gravel and dirt and sand, so when John's butt smacks that gravel, lots of dust blows up in the air and everybody out on that prison yard can see that dust—the Mexicans, the Whites, the Blacks, the Asians—and they all stop what they're doing. Then I hear one loud sound going all through that prison yard—*Whooaaaa!*

All the butt-kissers start saying, "John, you alright? You alright, man?" and they try to pick him up. John yells, "Let go of me!" but then he falls back down. Sandy says, "August, let's get out of here," and we take off across the yard.

At that point I have a lot of stuff to think about: *Man, I better go get my knife because I know I have to kill this guy when he comes at me! I know he won't just let this rest—I knocked him down right in front of the whole yard and I'm gonna have to kill this guy because this is the type of dude he is!*

So I go into a dorm. It isn't my dorm. It's just another dorm in the prison. All the inmates in there try to give me a knife. I tell them, "Man, I ain't carryin' no knife, because the officers know what happened and if they pull me up, they'll catch me with a knife and I'll pick up another case." In the meantime, John is all over the yard looking for me, with all his butt-kissers following behind him. But no one tells him where I am. It's crazy, man!

John Cole caught up with me the next morning at breakfast. Now, I know that it was nobody but the Lord that softened that dude's heart!

John said, "August, I was gonna kill you last night."

I said, "I'm just not gonna let you kill me."

He said, "Well, I *was* gonna kill you. But boy, you're lucky. I went to sleep and now I got a whole different frame of mind."

"Uh huh."

"But what you did to me was disrespectful."

I said, "What you did to *me* was disrespectful." John was listening now. "I told you I don't go for that playin' around. You know I don't want nobody puttin' his hands on me, man."

John quieted down. Then one of his butt-kissers tried to say something like, "Just let it go," and John slapped that guy hard—*POW!*—and told him, "Shut up! I didn't tell you to say nothin'." I thought, *Man, this guy is a piece of work.*

I know that God softened John Cole's heart that night, because I really would have had to kill this guy. But we resolved the situation and later we both got out of that prison. I never trusted him back in the neighborhood. He shot one of my homeboys in the back right after I got out of prison and paralyzed him.

John has been dead for fifteen years now. He was just an evil dude. Back then I was not walking with God, but I see today that God was always there for me. And that's just amazing to me now.

Everything is funny

Pookey was a bully. His dad lived across the street from me, so me and Pookey were cool. But Pookey ran with another bully named Sonny Boy. Me and Sonny Boy never got along. Never. He was bigger and I was younger, so he tried to bully me. One night someone killed Pookey, so that left Sonny Boy by himself in the neighborhood.

There was this burger place that I loved called the Three Deuces. It made the greasiest hamburgers! It had nice tables inside, or you could sit at this big U-shaped counter by the grill and eat your hamburger there.

One day I am in the Three Deuces and Sonny Boy comes in. Then—I forget why—Sonny Boy comes over to me and takes a swing at me. He connects with me, but he doesn't hit me good, so I clock him on the jaw and knock him over a table. Then I see something strange—Sonny Boy gets back up on his feet, he stands there holding his face with one hand, he looks at me, and I see that he is *crying!* Then he runs out the door. I stand there thinking, *Is this the bully I know?*

A little while later I am standing outside on the street, right where the street connects with an alley—I think it was 12th Street. All of a sudden, while I am standing there, this older woman runs up to me with a pistol in her hand. She is really mad, and she asks me, "Where's Big Dog at?" I'm thinking, *She's gonna shoot me*, so I tell her, "He just ran down that alley there," and I pointed. Then I said, "I shoudda *grabbed* him for ya!" So she goes running down that alley, and I start running the other way. I'm thinking, *She really WAS gonna shoot me!*

About a week later I'm at the Three Deuces again. I am sitting at the counter with my homeboys and I see Sonny Boy come through the door. Now, one side of that U-shaped counter—where I am sitting that day—is away from the door. The bottom of the U is on my right, where my homeboys are sitting. Sonny Boy sits down on the other side of that U-shaped counter, by the door, so that he is sitting straight across from me, but some ways away.

After Sonny Boy comes in, all my homeboys are looking at me like, *Hey Dog! There's Sonny Boy.* They are scared of Sonny Boy—he had these real long arms. But I already know that Sonny Boy doesn't want more problems with me, because I knocked him over that table. So I just nod my head at Sonny Boy and smile. When I smile at him, Sonny Boy looks at me real angry and doesn't say nothin' to me.

Everybody there at the Three Deuces is ordering hamburgers, because this place is famous for those greasy hamburgers. So I start wondering, *Mmm. Sonny Boy ain't saying nothin'. He ain't eatin' a burger. He's just got himself a soda and he's sucking on the straw.* I keep looking at Sonny Boy carefully. I smile at him again, and I keep smiling at him because I don't know what he's up to.

Then Sonny Boy says something to me, but I can't understand what he is saying. It was like mumbling. I say, "What'd you say, man?"

He says, "Ju shink evvy shing ish vunny, doan ju." But when Sonny Boy says that, his lips aren't moving.

I say, "What'd you say, Sonny Boy?"

"Ju shink evvy shing ish vunny."

I say, "What? I can't—"

"Ju shink evvy shing ish vunny!"

Now I see what's going on—Sonny Boy's jaw is wired shut! That's why he ain't eatin' no burger and he is suckin' on that soda! He is wired! I think, *Wow! I broke this dude's jaw!*

Eventually, I ended up dating Sonny Boy's niece. Whenever I went over to their family's house, Sonny Boy would talk trash to me. I would tell him, "Man, you are always runnin' your mouth. You need to be wired up again," and then I would go get his niece.

Drug houses

Even though I was a shotcaller for the gang, I started using cocaine myself—heavy. Those dealers had me strung out, way out there. I only had a year of that, but that was my worst year. To get drugs I would rob the drug houses where all the dope fiends were. They feared me.

I remember one time, I am sitting at a table in a house. I have a pistol in my hand and I have all the addicts that were in that house over in the corner, balled up on the floor. I have a pipe and I'm trying to smoke some crack. All those people I've got on the floor are scared to death because when you're smoking that stuff, it's like bustin' your head. That gun is in my hand but it's moving all around and I don't know which way it's pointing.

They say, "August, set the gun down!"

I say, "Shut up!"

"Just set the gun down."

"You just be quiet."

I kept them all piled up on each other over in the corner while I smoked some crack.

Another time, it is four or five o'clock in the morning and I am in this drug house trying to smoke some cocaine at the kitchen table and watch the news. There are these two crackheads in there with me, fighting with each other. One of them goes and gets a big ol' shotgun and they start yelling and when I look, they are standing there pulling back and forth on that shotgun. I also have a gun with me there—at that time I kept a 9mm Glock on me—but this is not a hostile environment where I don't have control. So I yell, "Hey! Put the gun down!" They look at me. I say, "Put the gun down, shut up and let me finish watching the news! Then you two can kill each other," and they listen to me. So here I am with these two dope fiends who are fighting over the last little piece of dope they have and there's a shotgun involved! I had to be crazy.

In another incident, I went to rob this guy at his house. I had robbed him twice already and I was high, trying to rob him again. I would go in through the bathroom window. This time he heard me, when I fell into the bathtub, and he came back there with a gun. I sat there in that bathtub and talked with him. I said, "Don't point that gun at me." Eventually I got the gun away from him and ended up robbing him with his own gun. It was strange.

I was caught up in so many bad situations when I was using drugs. But God was always there. 'Not giving me the green light to do what I was doing, because it was wrong. But God was trying to get me to a particular place in my life. So he had to protect me to get me there. With the stuff I went through, I'm amazed I made it.

Speedy

[Contribution by Pastor Lynwood "Speedy" Young, New Hope Church of Christ, Long Beach, California]

I wanna say this here—God knew what he was doin' with August. Let someone else tell you—me and him is supposed to be *dead!* It's God's grace. The mighty hand of *God* delivered us!

I grew up on the Eastside of Long Beach. When I was in the sixth grade, my mother moved us to the Westside where it was safe. But every summer I would visit my relatives on the Eastside and spend time there because I was accustomed to the excitement and activity. Over there you'd hear gun battles and high-speed chases with si-reens goin' off and helicopters flyin' over—*constantly*. It was like Viet Nam. The Westside wasn't like that.

I think I first met August when I was fifteen, about the tenth grade; he was a year younger. The two of us were close—when you saw one, you saw the other; that was before he met Trent. When my mother bought my school clothes, she would buy August his school clothes too. She bought him his first pair of Stacy Adams shoes, and back then you were *nothin'* 'til you had those Stacy Adams shoes.

When I turned eighteen, I started doin' my own thing on the Eastside. I got smoked out on drugs so bad. *Bad!* I mean, I was ashamed to go to my parents. I was ashamed to be around my relatives. You see, a smoker is the lowest thing on the earth. A smoker—he's like *nothin'!* Worse than a *dog!* That's the way people look at you when you're smokin' cocaine.

But August didn't forget what me and him went through. He didn't change one *bit* toward me. When it got cold, he made sure I had a big ol' jacket with a hood on it. He made sure I ate *e- ver- y day!* And many times he would give me about two hundred dollars worth of drugs and he would tell me, "Keep your sharp. Keep your hustle. Just bring me back thirty dollars," and I could survive by selling that on the streets.

But one time I messed up with the drugs; I messed up with what August gave me, right? I felt bad. I couldn't face him. But August sent a message out, "Tell Speedy that he ain't got to run from me. I got some more for him. Tell him to come get some more." That's homey-love right there.

Another time there was this guy, he would hang out over on Myrtle Avenue. I was selling drugs for August on Salt Lake Street, but customers would come over from Myrtle—which was about a block away—to buy from me. I had Myrtle sewed up—I mean, *sewed up!*—and that guy was mad about that. He wanted that territory.

Then one day I was in some drug house smokin', and that guy on Myrtle sent someone to go get me. He told him, "Go tell Speedy I want to buy a hundred dollars worth of drugs," but it was a setup. I ran over to Myrtle to see what he wanted. The guy took his fist and punched me hard in the face—like you would *do* to a smoker—and broke my glasses! I was knocked out for about ten seconds, and then I took off.

One of the other smokers there on Myrtle—this girl—she knew I worked for August, so she ran over to Salt Lake Street and told him what happened. It was raining that day and they told me that August got into his Seville—August had a brand new Cadillac Seville back then—and he took off and fishtailed around the corner goin' toward Myrtle, and when he got there he spotted the guy who punched me. Now, at that time August carried a pearl-handled, nickel-plated, 16-shot Taurus 9mm with a laser sight. August walked up on that guy and said, "Open up," and he jammed that 9mm in the guy's mouth and the guy went down on his *knees!* August said, "Let me tell you somethin'. Speedy's a smoker—sure enough! But that's one smoker you better *never* touch. As a matter of fact, I'm gonna give him a second sack of drugs and bring him over here to stand, and he better sell out in the next hour. You better not make *one sale!*" That's how August cared for me back then.

Another time when we were young—about seventeen or eighteen—it was nighttime and I was driving my '68 Cougar up the 110 freeway to LA. August was sittin' there next to me and we were so smoked-out on PCP that I had to stop that car right there in the middle lane so August could drive. I stopped the car and we both jumped out and we ran around the front of the car to switch places and the other cars were flyin' by us. *Man!*

But now we are both walkin' with the Lord.

There's no telling

One of the dope dealers I robbed got sent to jail for something he did, so he was an available witness against me. The DA told him that if he testifies against me—if he says I robbed him—they would cut him loose. He agreed, even though he knew he was taking a chance with his life, because he might end up being locked up in prison with me, someone he testified on. So my lawyer laid it out for me: "They'll give you ten years if you take this to trial." So I took a deal for three years in prison, because I knew the guy would testify against me.

When I was headed back to prison, I was shackled to my seat on the prison bus. That guy who was going to testify against me was on that same bus. He saw me sitting there with some of my homeboys and he said, "Man, I'm really sorry," because he knew I could have him "done" in prison. But I gave him a pass.

When I got there, I said to myself, *Here you are again, back in prison!* I was angry. But this time I was the shotcaller for all the Crips in there. We hooked up with the White gangs to do drug deals together, but a guy named Cowboy started disrespecting me on the deals. One day I caught him by himself in the corridor where our cells were and I beat him down real bad, but not bad enough to send him to the hospital. I knew the rules of the penitentiary: If you beat a guy, you better make sure you beat him bad enough to get him off the yard—you send him to the hospital—or else he'll come back and get you. But I didn't do that, because Cowboy and I were friends at first.

A few days later I am walking from the prison kitchen, across the yard. I have just got off work and I am headed for the building where my cell is. In front of that building, out in the yard, is a little shack where they keep the baseball equipment, and in there they have a little store where you can buy ice cream, candy—things like that. So I am walking toward that little shack to get to my building. All of sudden Cowboy pops out from behind that shack.

Cowboy works with packages in the prison, so he says, "August. I got a package for you."

I think, *He doesn't have no package for me*, and I say, "You don't owe me no package, Cowboy."

Cowboy says, "Oh yeah I do," and he starts walking toward me. I am watching him, because I don't know if he's got a knife. I see these trash cans just to my left and I think, *If he pulls a knife, I'll grab one of those trash lids and crown him king.*

But Cowboy is actually diverting my attention while one of his guys comes up behind me, so right then I feel *that* guy stab me in my lower back, where my kidneys are. I spin around and see the guy and swing at *him*. Then Cowboy stabs me in my back with a bedspring that they had straightened out and sharpened like an ice pick, so I spin around again and swing at him. They have stabbed me twice!

Cowboy takes off across the yard. The other guy runs into a building. I grab one of the bats from that shack and start running after Cowboy, but I forget about the gun tower. Some of my homeboys are right there playing baseball and they all yell, "August!" and I stop. Someone says, "He's gonna shoot you." I look up and I see a guard in the gun tower looking at me through binoculars. I drop the bat.

Cowboy and some other guys head into the sergeant's office. I go and wait out in front, and then my homeboys come around.

They say, "Man, let's go in and get 'em!"

I say, "I'm gonna wait out here."

"Come on! You're not scared?"

"No, but I'm not stupid. Wait 'til they come out."

I am bleeding bad now. My homeboys try to fix me up, so that the blood doesn't draw attention. They place shirts and stuff on my back. I am sitting there waiting, and one of the officers—a young guy—comes over and talks with me. I tell him, "Naw, man. Everything's cool."

Finally I go up to my cell. But right after I get there, a bunch of officers come and get me out. As I'm walking down the corridor, some White guys that I know from those drug deals start yelling from their cells, "We shoudda killed you! We shoudda killed you!" but I don't talk back to them because I don't want the goon squad there. The officers take me to the hole and handcuff me in there. Before long, I am puking on the floor. I get the chills. I am dying in there, because my kidneys are poisoned.

After a day in the hole, the officers looked at me and I was not moving. They rushed me to the hospital on the outside. I stayed there three days. They gave me a spinal tap—I think—to see if something got into my blood. After three days, I got sent back to the prison.

The prison tried to convince me to go to court on the guys who stabbed me. But I would not do that. I *could* not do that. All my homeboys would say, "Dude, you told on them?" That's the way it is in prison. Even though those guys stabbed me, there's no telling. So the goon squad got mad at me because I wouldn't tell on those guys, and threw me back in the hole.

I stayed in the hole a couple months. It was scary. It was scary that I was alone, in one small cell. No windows. In the daytime they turn the ceiling light on, but they only leave that light on for a short time, so you are always in darkness, alienated from the world. You know what I'm saying? There were other inmates who were in the hole, in their cells dying. I mean, the guards were taking them out of there dead, and I was watching.

When I got out of the hole, they sent me to a minimum security area across the street from the main prison. I had to spend another two months there before they would send me home.

That was my first time ever in the hole. And it was the first time I ever got stabbed in prison. I almost didn't make it out of that place. It was Hell. I see now how the Lord was with me. He allowed me to come out of there.

A visitor!

> *But while he was still a long way off, his father saw him and was filled with compassion for him; he ran to his son, threw his arms around him and kissed him.*

Luke 15

One day I am laying on my bunk in the prison dorm, about midmorning. I have finished lifting weights out at the prison weight pile, and I am worn out. A guard that I know comes into the dorm, walks over by me and kicks my bunk.

He says, "Get up. You've got a visitor."

This guard likes to joke, so I say, "Get away from my bunk."

"No. Listen. You got a visitor."

"Nobody comes to see me."

"You got a—"

"Stop playin' with me!"

"I'm telling you. You need to get up and get ready and go to your visit."

I look at him. "You're serious."

"I'm serious."

I get up and get dressed, because no one has ever come to see me the whole time I have been in prison and I only had gotten two letters and I am thinking, *Who would come see a nobody like me?*

I walk out of the dorm, into the yard, get my visitor pass and walk up to a gate. The guards let me through. They tell me to head for this one building they point to. In there they strip me down naked and search me. I put my clothes back on and they release me through a door into this big visitor room.

In the visitor room I see tables and chairs and all kinds of visitors sitting there. I see other inmates I know—guys I lift weights with, guys I gangbang with—all in there visiting with their families. I stand there looking at everything. They see me and say, "Hey Big Dog. What's up?" I know these guys come there every weekend. But this is all new for me.

I know that the guards don't allow your visitors to come into the room until you get there, so I sit down. I sit and wait. I wonder who it is. I think, *Is this a joke? Did they just call me out here to make me look like a fool?* I wait and wait.

All of a sudden the guard pulls open the visitor door and I see my dad. It's my *dad!* He's older, but it's him! He is wearing a suit and tie. I notice my cousin behind him—his sister's daughter—and then some elderly woman, and for a second I think, *Who is this lady?* But mostly I am stunned that it's my dad. I stand up. My heart is pounding. My dad walks over to me with a big smile and says, "Son!" and that word strikes me hard! We hug. He says, "August, you done got big!" I am holding back the tears. I'm feeling, *Here's my dad all the way from New Orleans, so he must love me.* We sit down at a table. He tells me how he loves me, and I settle down.

I wonder, *Who is this lady?* I'm thinking she's one of my aunties, one of my dad's older sisters. Then my dad says, "This is my wife." He is a pastor by then. I eventually found out that the church that he is operating at that time, together with this wife, is full of what I call "church-kidnapping people" where you go to church about eight o'clock on Sunday morning and you can't get out of there until three o'clock in the afternoon, and you better come back later that night. That's church-kidnapping.

Then my dad tells me, "Son, I had a hard time finding you here in prison. But I wouldn't give up. I'm mad at your mother's family. They told me you were locked up, but none of them would help me find you. I told them, 'He's locked up right there by you and none of y'all are going to visit him?' So I had to come out here myself. God laid you on my heart, August. I love ya so much!" I know for a fact that my mom's family just didn't want to deal with my dad.

When I was growing up, all the other kids had dads. I didn't have a dad. That's how I got hooked up with gangs. Whenever I thought about my dad, it was, *Man, I'll kill that dude.* I carried that hate around with me my whole life, up until that day. But that day, all I know is—my dad came all the way from New Orleans to visit me and we never talked like this before. At that point, all that bad stuff is gone and a relationship is starting right there. I am thinking, *I'll go back to New Orleans to make a relationship with my dad.*

We talk for a couple hours. We keep hugging. We discuss lots of stuff— I can't remember it all. My cousin keeps interrupting and his wife says something now and then. But I have a nice visit with my dad. Then it's four o'clock and everyone has to go. The inmates sit in there until all the visitors go out a big metal door and the guard closes it. Then we go out a different door.

When I go to get stripped down again, I am still in shock. *It was my dad that came.* While we're all getting dressed, the other inmates are talking, but I am quiet. I walk back to the dorm, just thinking the whole way.

Later, I am laying on my bunk looking at the ceiling. *What made him come here?* I promise myself, *When I get out of this prison, I'm gonna try to draw close to my dad.* And when the time came, I did try. But I came to learn, my dad was an off-and-on type of dude.

Chapter 3 Study Guide

Jailhouse justice

As the older guy found out at the trial, it is difficult to manipulate circumstances to avoid guilt, especially in the long run. Whether it is through authorities like the DA or members of the community like the other men in the jail, justice tends to find its way into our lives. This is a practical rule for daily living. But as Christians we also believe that we will one day face God's eternal righteousness and justice. Have you ever been treated unfairly, only to have things work out alright in the end? Are you denying justice in any way—big or small—to anyone around you?

I'm gonna have to kill this guy!

We all have boundaries around us that protect us—physical, emotional, psychological or spiritual boundaries. If you respect and love a person, you will respect their boundaries. Otherwise you run the risk of having them exclude you from their life. In the heat of the moment you may disrespect someone's boundaries, because those boundaries go against what you want. But if you care about a person, you will repair any damage and reestablish respect. God can intervene, as he did with John Cole, to clarify our own thinking about the boundaries of others, so that an issue can be resolved. In this story, that intervention saved a life, either August's or John's. What boundary do you allow others to violate? Why do you fail to protect yourself? What is in your heart that has caused you to step over someone else's boundaries?

Everything is funny

When we face a bully in life—an unfair boss, a harsh parent, a critical spouse, a self-righteous friend, a nasty coworker—we should give ourselves permission to say to ourselves, *When it comes to you, "evvy shing ish vunny."* Why do we take bullies so seriously? Why are we afraid of them? Why give power to a fool? See them for what they really are, and smile. Who have you needlessly feared? Who is the bully in your life?

Drug houses

A life out of control can put us in desperate situations. The hope of the Christian faith is that even when we are at our worst—whether by intention or by circumstance—God is hard at work to redeem us. If we let Him, He uses our experiences and our talents to teach us and preserve us, on our way to the better things He has for us. Our prayer each day should be to discern His actions in our lives. Are you, figuratively speaking, waving a "gun" to terrorize (control) those around you? Is your house in some way as chaotic as the houses in the story? Is God protecting you, to get you to the place where you should be?

Speedy

Whatever Speedy and August had been through together—before Speedy developed his drug problem—it gave them a deep sense of affection and loyalty. At a time when August had power, he protected Speedy, who was especially vulnerable. To August, Speedy was not a "dog" or "nothin'." August treated Speedy as "somebody," and that attitude sent both men down the path toward redemption. Do you have the power to protect someone who needs your help? Do you, at least in your thinking, treat someone like a dog? Have you ever been powerless and had someone reach out to you to help?

There's no telling

Many people understand, especially looking back on life, that God has carried them through bad circumstances. We can create those circumstances ourselves, or the world can impose them on us. In the middle of those circumstances we can forget that God is with us. It is important to remember those glimpses of God we get when we face trouble. We can spare ourselves having to relearn the lesson that God is faithful. You are always under His watchful eye and care. When has it felt like you were all alone, only to find out that God was there all the time? Have you ever dug yourself in a hole and discovered that God was there to provide a way out?

A visitor!

We should be prepared for God to shock us out of our routine. A bad situation in our lives can go on for years, and desperation and hopelessness can set in. But God is in control, and His timing is perfect. Things can change suddenly for the better if we are open to God's plan. No matter what prison we are in—hopelessness, poverty, despair, fearfulness—a "visit" can occur suddenly and change our point of view. Are you currently stuck, or somehow in despair? Do you need a "visit" in your life to give you hope? Do you look for one?

Chapter 4 – Return to New Orleans

Return visit

*Jethro was delighted to hear about all the good things the Lord had
done for Israel in rescuing them from the hand of the Egyptians.*

Exodus 18

After my dad visited me, I got out of the penitentiary for the second time. At first, I went back to the neighborhood and the gangs. They gave me drugs to sell, and a lot of money. So I took my son and my nephew and we got on a flight to New Orleans, to spend time with my dad.

When I got to New Orleans, my dad and I talked a lot. It was amazing to have a dad, because I always wanted that love from a male perspective. One day we were having lunch together at this little place, and there was a woman in there eating. She was Creole—green eyes—beautiful. My dad said, "She sure is looking at you." Later I went into the men's room and when I came out she was standing there and we bumped together. I said, "I'm sorry." She said, "What's your name?" and she gave me her phone number. I called her for a date and my dad drove me there. He told her, "This is my son. I don't want anything to happen to him." That impressed me. It turned out, she was married to a policeman and getting a divorce and I didn't want none of *that!* But I remembered what my dad said to her.

My dad asked me if I would let him baptize me. I knew it was right to be baptized and I knew it was right for him to ask me, because he was a pastor. I said, "Yeah. Sure." He baptized me and my son and my nephew in the name of Jesus. At that time, I did not understand the significance of baptism, but it was a good feeling. I realize now that *that* moment changed my whole life, all the way up to today. Long Beach, for me, was like Egypt was for the children of Israel. God delivered them out of Egypt where they had nothing but trouble and slavery. In the same way, God had delivered me out of Long Beach when I went down to New Orleans to see my dad.

But I left New Orleans after being with my dad for only two weeks, and I went back to Long Beach—to Egypt. God had delivered me out of there, but it was my plan to go right back into what I had been doing there—selling drugs and runnin' with the gangs.

So God started dealing with me back there in Long Beach. It took another five or six years for Him to finish the work, but right then God started snippin' stuff out of my life, little by little. Big money, drugs, power in the gangs—He started snippin' all that away, bit by bit. I knew something was going on, but I did not want to admit it. I loved being in the gangs. I loved the way I was brought up—sellin' drugs, gamblin', doing it the street way.

For the next six years, I ran from God, back deep into the gangs. I didn't understand until later, you cannot run from Him.

Tick Tock

> *Goliath stood and shouted to the ranks of Israel, "Why do you come out and line up for battle? Am I not a Philistine, and are you not the servants of Saul? Choose a man and have him come down to me." ... David said to Saul, "Let no one lose heart on account of this Philistine; your servant will go and fight him."*

1 Samuel 17

After I got out of the penitentiary the second time, in 1986, and after that trip to New Orleans to see my dad, I didn't fit into the gangs right away. I had to wait for my piece of the action to come. I knew I would get back into the money some way. Somebody was going to give. It just wasn't going to happen—that everybody in that neighborhood had money and I didn't have any. But for the time being, I got my money by running the dice games on Pasadena Avenue, and I just kept pressuring all the gangsters there.

My cousin Cat Man operated around the corner, on Elm Avenue. He was already out of prison for a while, and he was selling a lot of the drugs in the neighborhood. But he wasn't sharing with me, and that made me mad. I had a talk with him and I told him, "Why do *you* got everything? You're not sharin' with me."

Cat Man had a guy working for him named Tick Tock. I called Tick Tock "Sasquatch," because he weighed about four hundred pounds. But he wasn't lean. He was a fat eater. You know what I mean?

Tick Tock had attitude. He would *smash* on people. Just *crack* 'em! He would bully the youngsters in the Rollin' 20's Crips, so they didn't like Tick Tock. I didn't like Tick Tock either. He was big, but as far as I was concerned, he better stay out of my way, because I was big too. By that time I was bench pressing five hundred pounds. I was strong. I had power in my chest and arms.

My cousin Cat Man had Tick Tock selling crack, even though Tick Tock was from the other gang. Tick Tock could bully the other sellers. Whatever territory Tick Tock was selling drugs on, nobody else would sell drugs there. So my cousin was making big money off of Tick Tock.

But then one day, Tick Tock finally went after Cat Man. I was around the corner on Pasadena Avenue and some guy came running to get us. He said, "Hey man! Your cousin and Tick Tock are gonna get into it!" I said, "What?" and I started runnin' to help my cousin.

There was this little guy that ran over there with me, Darryl Mackbee. Mackbee loved to hang around with me. Any time I got into an altercation with somebody, he would stand off to the side and laugh. One time I asked him, "Mackbee, why every time I get into it with somebody, you start laughin'?" He said, "Man, 'cause I know what's fixin' to happen." He knew I would knock 'em out. He knew I would put 'em to sleep. And that made Mackbee laugh.

So that day, me and Mackbee come running around the corner on Elm Avenue. I see the situation—Tick Tock and Big Cat are about to get into it. I say, "You know Mackbee, my cousin won't let me in on things. I'm just gonna see how he handles this guy on his own. This is a big dude." I'm thinking my cousin can handle Tick Tock alright, because my cousin is a mean piece of work. But this dude is big. Me and Mackbee stand there while Tick Tock and Big Cat argue back and forth. Tick Tock wants my cousin to pay him more money.

Cat Man says, "Yeah?"

Tick Tock says, "Yeah, or I'll whoop your ass!"

I think, *Wow!* I say to my cousin, "Are you gonna let him talk to you like that?"

Cat man says, "August, just be quiet."

I say, "Ffff! What do you mean, 'Just be quiet?' You need to tell *him* to be quiet."

Then Tick Tock looks at me. He says, "Who's this? I'll knock him out too."

I turn to Tick Tock and I say, "You'll do *what* brother?"

He tells me, "I'll put my hands on you."

"Man, you are not doin' *nothin'* to me. You have better action in my cousin there."

"Oh! Cat Man's your cousin? Then I'll knock you both out!"

I say, "Well, come on. Bring it." Mackbee starts laughing. Tick Tock comes at me, swings and misses, and I clock him on the jaw. He goes down to the ground. He is out cold.

So now Tick Tock is snoring out there in the middle of the street. I grab on to him and drag him off to the side, so he doesn't get run over by a car. His homeboys are saying, "Don't kill him Dog!" I say, "I am not gonna kill him," and I pull him up and put him up against a car. "But he is gonna know who I am," and—*POOM!*—I slap him with my hand, hard. That cuts his face all open, because I have these serious calluses on my palms from lifting weights.

While I'm holding him up against the car, Tick Tock starts waking up. He says, "What's happenin'?"

His homeboys tell him, "Be quiet. Don't say nothin'."

"Did he knock me out?"

I'm still hangin' on to him, and I say, "Yeah, I did. And you're about ready for another one," and—*POW!*—I clock him on the jaw again. He goes right back to sleep. I let him fall to the ground. Then I search through his pockets and take all his money. I stand up. Then I look at my cousin. I see Mackbee laughing. I say, "Darryl, you have *got* to stop laughin' at these people."

After that day, whenever Tick Tock would see me, he'd say, "How ya doin' August?" because he respected me. But I found out later what was really happening. After that day when I knocked out Tick Tock, whatever spot I was selling drugs at, that other gang would always come around at night and shoot at me. Years after that, when I was out of the gangs and was walking with the Lord, one of those boys called me.

He said, "Remember when you would get shot at?"

I said, "Yeah."

"And remember when somebody drove by and you were walkin' out of that gate and you jumped behind a car real fast and the gun didn't go off until they got down the street and *then* the gun went off?"

"Yeah."

"Well, that was Tick Tock."

"That was Tick Tock?"

"Yeah man."

I said, "I didn't know that." It was him all the time. During the day he would be around me, but at night he was trying to kill me, and I never knew it.

Then that boy told me, "Well, they killed Tick Tock last night."

"Who did?"

"Those youngsters. They smoked him."

"Where?"

"Right by the statue."

That was at King's Park, where we all hung out. It has a Martin Luther King statue just off the parking lot.

The strange thing is, that's right where Mackbee got shot too. Just a short time after I knocked out Tick Tock, I was at home with my girl, and Mackbee came over with a guy named Kool Aid. My girl had made some chicken, some mashed potatoes, some greens. Mackbee, Kool Aid and me were drinking Hennessy and smoking marijuana, but I was not accustomed to that, being just out of prison. Mackbee and Kool Aid stood up to go to King's Park, but my girl told me, "You're not leaving! Not like that." "Okay," I said. "You guys go ahead."

Then Mackbee and Kool Aid drove into the parking lot at King's Park. As soon as they got out of the car, two other guys with shotguns came up right there by 'em; one of *their* homeboys had got jumped there that day and the two guys with shotguns were looking for the ones that did it, and they found Kool Aid and Mackbee. Those two guys each chambered a round in those shotguns—*SHA-SHAK! SHA-SHAK!* One of them yelled, "We're gonna kill y'all!" then, *BOOM! BOOM!* Kool Aid died. They blowed

Mackbee's guts out, but he healed. When I heard what happened, I thought, *Good thing I listened to my girl.*

My dog Noodles

So I began selling drugs again—big time—and I bought myself a little pit bull puppy. I got him when his eyes first opened. He was brown, with green eyes and a red nose. I named him Noodles.

I don't know how Noodles got to be so *mean*. When Noodles was still a puppy, I would take him to King's Park. The girls would come by to admire him and Noodles would start sniffing their ankles. They'd say, "Aw, he's so cute," then before too long, "Wait. Wait! What's he doing? Ah!" and Noodles would start chewing on their ankles and I would have to grab him. I took Noodles to the vet because he was losing his baby teeth from biting everybody. The vet made a special muzzle for him because you can't buy a muzzle for a dog that small. And I had his ears clipped.

When Noodles got older, I took him everywhere. No one could get close to me. If someone at the park let me hold their little child, I could not set that child down, because Noodles would try to eat that child. At the park, if some kid ran over by me, I couldn't let that kid then just run off on his own, because after Noodles saw that kid with me he'd try to chase him down and chew him up.

Whenever I left town, my mom would take care of Noodles. Back then I drove a 1966 Malibu HL—eggshell white with blue-pearl finish—with 520s and Dayton wires. Whenever I drove that Malibu up to my mom's house after being out of town, Noodles would hear that car coming with the music on, and when I would pull into my mom's driveway I could see him looking out through the screen door, crying real loud—*AAR! AAR! AAR!*—and my mom would open the screen door for him and Noodles would come running out and jump right through the open passenger window of my Malibu and start lickin' on me. One time we did that, but then my mom walked out of the house and leaned through that window to ask me a question and Noodles chomped down on her arm and I had to grab Noodles and pry his mouth open and rush my mom to the hospital. This was my dog, you know? He was downright mean!

Around that time, me and some of my homeboys migrated to San Diego, to sell drugs for a while. The San Diego gangs hated us. They'd see my white Malibu and say, "Those LA boys are here again."

In San Diego, there was this apartment building on Gloria Street that was run by a crackhead woman who had kids, and there was another lady inside there selling drugs. So we just took over the whole apartment building. Then we took the crackheads that were around there—just a few of them— and we put them outside the apartment building selling drugs, so that our customers did not have to come to the door. We sent those crackheads out onto the street with only a little crack at a time, because sometimes they would run off.

We were making maybe five thousand dollars a day there in San Diego. We would come down from Long Beach and be there from Monday through Sunday morning. Then we would go back to Long Beach on Sunday, come back Monday and stay the whole week again. We were doing that on an ongoing basis.

Whenever we were at that apartment building in San Diego, I would be sitting at the kitchen table, cutting up the crack. We would use half a kilo at a time and just cut it all up and bag it. Noodles would be under the table at my feet, on a leash, so that he could come out only so far. By that time Noodles was real big, and mean as the Devil! The only ones he would respect was me and one of my other homeboys.

One day in San Diego, I am napping in the bedroom at the apartment and I wake up hearing some girl hollerin' real loud. I come out of the bedroom and there's my homeboy and I say, "What's goin' on?" and he yells, "I caught her! I caught her!" and then there's more hollerin' from the kitchen and I hurry in there and see blood all over the front of the refrigerator and the floor, and I see this crackhead standing there handcuffed to the refrigerator door screaming her head off and Noodles is chewing up her legs.

I go get Noodles off her and I ask my homeboy, "Man, what did you do?"

"She ran off!"

I said, "You can't do this, man."

"Well—"

"She'll tell, and then we are done here."

So I take the girl and have one of the other crackheads rush her to the hospital. We gave her a little crack, so she was cool. She still came around after that.

The fish market

They saw a fire of burning coals there with fish on it, and some bread. ... Jesus said to them, "Come and have breakfast."

John 21

When I was in the gangs, I had friends that totally disagreed with me, totally did not understand me, totally judged me. But they were still my friends.

These friends needed to see reality. The gangs were my world. It was a crazy world, and as I got older I *knew* it was crazy. But they couldn't comprehend that world. When I told them stories about the gangs, it would really mess them up. But after a while, they'd tell me, "Since I've gotten to know you, I see you're not a bad person." I'd say, "Well, hey brother, that makes me feel good!" and I would laugh. They had judged me by what they heard. Jesus told us not to judge, because we will be judged the same way. We need to be careful about that.

There is a fish market in Long Beach called the Pee & Gee Fish Market, on Martin Luther King Avenue. It's in a little mall. The VIP record store is on one side, where Snoop Dogg got his start, and on the other side is a church pastored by my homeboy Glenn Lassiter.

The Pee & Gee Fish Market is owned by my friend Hussein. Hussein is from Lebanon. He is an honest guy, and when I first met him—I was in the gangs at that time—Hussein already had other businesses in Lebanon. He bought the Pee & Gee Fish Market from Mr. Green, who owned it for many years when we were young. Hussein married a woman in my neighborhood and they had a son—oh how he loved that baby boy!

Right after Hussein bought the fish market, people in that neighborhood came against him. They would say, "This is our fish market!" They would come in there and just *harass* Hussein. All the gangsters hung out right there in the parking lot and Hussein had these big storefront windows and those gangsters would just bust out those windows and come in there and talk crazy to Hussein.

So Hussein was a wreck when I finally talked to him. I think someone at the VIP told Hussein, "Talk to August. They call him 'Big Dog.' His cousin is 'Cat Man.' He's got control over those guys." So one day when I went in there to buy fish, Hussein took the time to talk to me.

Hussein told me, "Yes-yes-yes! I know Tony."

I said, "You know Cat Man?"

"Tony is my good friend."

"Oh yeah?"

"Yes. I helped him out one time."

We kept talking, and me and Hussein became good friends. The gangsters backed off of him, and they would actually come into the Pee &

Gee, spend money, sit down and eat and respect Hussein. Whenever I went in there with my boys, they would ask me, "Why do we gotta pay and you don't?" I'd say, "You be quiet, man." Years later, Hussein's son got in trouble in the gangs and I helped him with that.

If Hussein had not got in trouble with the fish market, he never would have come down to my level. He wouldn't have ever talked to me, because he was living a high life. You know what I'm saying? But he got put in a position where he had to communicate with me, or he would have been out of business. He had to face the reality of where he was—all those people and gangsters comin' against him. With the situation he was in, he needed my help. And we became friends.

Violated

> *Then the Philistines seized Sampson, gouged out his eyes and took him down to Gaza. Binding him with bronze shackles, they set him to grinding in the prison.*
>
> *Judges 16*

In 1987 I was on parole from my second time in prison. But then I got violated.

I am at a club in Long Beach, standing at the bar. This girl I know starts talking to me. I say, "Get out of here girl," but then she throws her drink in my face. It burns my eyes and I can hear people laughing. I think, *Okay. Just wait 'til I get my sight back.*

I grab that girl, wrap her hair around my hand, walk her over to the window and throw her outside. Her little Puerto Rican friend runs up and cusses me out, so I throw *her* outside. Then some little guy hits me in the back of the head and about fifteen of my homeboys rush in and beat him down. They go ahead and snatch the cash register and tear up the whole club. My cousin gets arrested after running away across the tops of all the police cars, but I get out of there.

The Special Services Unit came to get me a couple weeks later. They pick up parolees, and they had been following me. On the day they pick me up, they watch me when I leave home to go to my mom's house. They follow me there. When I get out of the car, they come at me from both corners of the block. "Don't move! Lay down!" I think, *Wow!* They handcuff me, I get up, they put me in their car and they take me back to my house.

We are standing outside my front door and one guy asks me, "Is there anybody inside?"

I tell him, "Ain't nobody in there."

"If there is, we'll shoot."

"Like I said, ain't nobody in there."

"You'll get it first!"

Then I say, "What's up with *that*, dude?"

"There really isn't anybody in there?"

"My kid's at school. His mom's at work."

They take my key and open the door and they use me like a shield when we rush in there, me and about ten officers from the SSU. They tear up my house looking for drugs. They find a little steel box and I give them the key and they find twenty thousand dollars in cash in there. But they don't find drugs at my place, because I know not to keep drugs and money in the same place.

They say, "Robbing dope dealers again?"

"I don't rob."

"Selling drugs?"

"I don't sell drugs."

"Where'd you get this money?"

"I been savin' my money."

They can't just take the money for no reason, so they go into my son's room and they find a toy gun, and they come out and tell me, "This is a simulated weapon!"

"Man, that's a cap gun."

"No, it's a simulated weapon!"

"Ffff."

"You're robbing dope dealers again. We're taking you in."

So they violated me on my parole, with a cap gun. But they gave my money back. I told my girl, "I'm gone for a year. Take that money. Get what you need." I was just getting ready to get off parole, and this happens.

Making peace

> *Or suppose a king is about to go to war against another king. Will he not first sit down and consider whether he is able with ten thousand men to oppose the one coming against him with twenty thousand? If he is not able, he will send a delegation while the other is still a long way off and will ask for terms of peace.*

Luke 14

While I was waiting for my parole hearing, they sent me to a prison called CIM-East—California Institution for Men, East Facility—in Chino. About the time I got there, there was overcrowding in all the California prisons, so they sent inmates there from all over the state. A lot of them had come from Folsom and San Quentin after the big riots there between the Blacks and the Mexicans. It was a mad house! There were constant riots on the yard.

I became the leader of the Crips in there. That was huge! We would all walk the track together. Everybody in there, from every gang, knew that the Crips were big on that yard.

Then I found out something. The last time I was in prison, there was that White guy who stabbed me in my back—not Cowboy, but the other guy.

And that guy's cellmate was the one mouthin' off to me after I got stabbed, when he was yelling, "We shoudda killed you!" I wanted to *get* him back then, but I couldn't. And now, there he is on the yard at CIM-East. He sees me and I see him, and he knows the rules of the penitentiary: He is getting ready to get his head took off!

There were lots of ways I could have gotten this guy, and he knew it. One way was—see, to come out of a building there, an inmate would have to walk down a concrete ramp, a ramp like you would push a wheelchair down. And those ramps had concrete walls along both sides that were about chest high and tapered down. So you could hide behind those walls and peek over to see who was coming down the ramp. At that time we could lift weights in prison, and some inmates would take a dumbbell—a big one, like a thirty- or forty-pound dumbbell—and they would wait behind that wall until another inmate came down that ramp and then they would just slam the dumbbell down on top of his head. That would kill a guy, no problem.

So this guy wanted to talk to me right away. He knew I couldn't talk to him when all my homeboys were right there by me; my homeboys would have killed him if I just nodded my head. So he sent somebody over with a big balloon full of marijuana to tell me, "Hey, this is what I'm gettin' in here."

I had already decided in my heart that I wasn't going to hurt this guy, even before he sent anybody over to me. I don't know why. I didn't want that on my hands. I didn't want that on my mind. I couldn't see myself doing that to the guy, even though they tried to kill me. To be honest, I didn't have it in me to kill.

That guy finally came and talked to me. I told him, "You got nothin' to worry about. I'm not trippin'. But I don't want you around me." I couldn't let my homeboys know what I decided, because they would have done something to me. So I just let that go and never brought it up again. But the guy kept those balloons coming.

While I was at CIM-East, one of my homeboys started a big riot. I thought, *Man, I need to stay away from this stuff,* because there was a chance that those girls that I threw out the window at the bar would not show up at my parole hearing and I could get out early. But as it turned out, those girls did show up, and my parole violation was official.

So I was sent to another prison, CMC-West—California Men's Colony-West Facility. That's where I was the time my dad came to visit me, and where Cowboy stabbed me. I ran the Crips there again, but the Bloods were big there too. One time they came to me and said, "Man, deal with your homeboy One Round. He's sweatin' us over here in the dorm." I took care of that for them. I got into it with one of the Bloods at CMC-West because he had a smart mouth. I beat him down with a chair and broke his arm. I ran through the yard to get all my stuff, because I knew the prison would be coming after me. They called me on the loud speaker, *AUGUST HUNTER, REPORT TO THE SERGEANT'S OFFICE!* I didn't report and they swarmed the yard and got me back in the hole, across the street at CMC-East. That was that same hole where I almost died when Cowboy stabbed me. I was back in that same death trap.

I did three months extra for breaking that guy's arm. I thought, *That's it! I'm not coming back to the penitentiary. I am through with this!*

"Little Dog"

This kid Saddu was a youngster in the gang. My family knew him. He was a kid that came from Africa and moved to our neighborhood and became a full-fledged gang member. He just sold out!

In the gangs, every OG has a young G under him that represents him. Saddu wanted that position under me. He wanted to imitate the role I had in the gang. I was "Big Dog" and he wanted to be "Little Dog." But I wouldn't allow anyone to represent me.

Then there was another little homeboy in the gang. I think his name was Trey. I liked him. Trey wanted to sell drugs, but I wouldn't give him drugs to sell, because Trey was a little slow. If I had given him drugs to sell, he would have gone out there and caught a case and gone to jail. I told Trey, "You don't need to sell drugs. Just kick back." So Trey just hung out with me. But Saddu did not like that Trey and I were close.

Since the Rollin' 20's Crips wouldn't give Trey drugs to sell, he went and switched gangs—to the Insane Crips. They gave him a big ol' sack of drugs to sell and he was happy with that. But the youngsters in the gangs, they've got a thing about somebody changing gangs. As far as they are concerned, you can't be switching sides. If they hear about one of the homeys switching sides, that's big! So word got out that Trey did that, and Saddu wanted a reputation.

One day some of the young homeys are sitting in a car on the street where I hang out. It is the middle of the day. My homegirl Beebee is in the front seat, because it is her car. She has another one of my homeboys up front with her. Trey is sitting in the backseat. They are just talking to all the other homeboys and homegirls who are out on the street. They are all Rollin' 20's Crips, except that Trey is with the Insane Crips now.

Saddu walks up to the car and says, "How ya doin', Beebee?"

"Hey Saddu. How you doin'?"

Then Saddu goes to the back window and says, "Trey. I heard you're from Insane now."

Trey says, "Oh yeah, I'm from Insane now." Then Saddu takes a .38 Special out of his belt, puts it on Trey's chest and *blasts* him three times. *BOOM! BOOM! BOOM!* He just blowed Trey away in front of everybody! In the backseat of that car!

That incident messed Beebee up. She told me what she saw when she turned around and looked at Trey in the backseat. It was sad too, because Trey was just a little slow guy.

Saddu only did six years for that murder, because they really couldn't prove it. People knew, but nobody told. All they could squeeze out of him was eleven years, and he did six.

When Saddu came home from prison, he saw how I was. He saw that I was looking at things differently.

I said to Saddu, "What was you thinkin', man?"

"But Big Dog, he traded sides!"

"So what?"

"He can't play both ends!"

"Does that matter that much?"

"He was from our gang!"

I could see Saddu didn't like was I was saying, so I asked him, "Did you ask God to forgive you?"

He said, "Dog, don't push that stuff on me!" then, "Big Dog, you changed."

"Yeah, I have."

"You ain't Big Dog no more."

"No. I'm August."

He said, "Man!" and ran off, mad at me. He started beating up the other youngsters on the block where I lived.

Later I heard that one day Saddu made plans to meet his girl to go shopping. This day was hot—100 degrees. He met his girl and they went downtown shopping and he dropped dead. Cold dead.

I talked to my baby brother Jason about it. I said, "That's weird how Saddu dropped dead."

Jason told me, "Man, Saddu was comin' over here every day since he got out of prison, just sittin' here, drinkin'. That murder was eatin' him up."

"I kinda realized that."

"Man, that's all he would talk about. I finally told him, 'I don't want to hear no more.'"

I wish Saddu had listened to me.

My mom's ride by

Let's lie in wait for someone's blood, let's waylay some harmless soul.

Proverbs 1

When I ran the gang, I could not stand a bully. The young guys who got bullied, they knew they could come to me and I would give them a fair shake. I was not low-down. And that made the bullies mad.

Plus, I was a boxer. I was real quick with my fists. I could really put hands on people. So those bullies were never gonna go from the shoulder with me! No, that wasn't gonna happen!

So they would try to shoot us, me and my buddy Trent. They would sneak up and do ride-bys on us. There were so many shooting incidents. They were trying to kill us all the time. I'm telling you, people would shoot at me point blank and miss me, or the gun would not fire. They never were successful. They started calling me and Trent the "Untouchables."

So what those guys did is—they shot my mom. My mom worked at a doughnut shop. She would get off work at twelve o'clock at night and walk home five or six blocks. And one night they shot her. They did a ride-by on her when she was crossing the street. They shot her in the lower back.

That messed me up bad. They shot my mom, man!

How ya doin'?

> *For God does speak—now one way, now another—though man may not perceive it. In a dream, in a vision of the night, when deep sleep falls on men as they slumber in their beds, he may speak in their ears and terrify them with warnings, to turn man from wrongdoing and keep him from pride, to preserve his soul from the pit, his life from perishing by the sword.*
>
> *Job 33*

Then these guys I know shot at my car when I had my twin baby girls inside. Man! It's on now! I am *not* goin' for this one! When I see those guys, it's the Gunfight at the OK Corral—on sight! I'll go to the penitentiary for the rest of my life if I have to.

I called my dad. He said, "You know what?"

"What?"

"If you're gonna walk with God, you've got to forgive those guys."

I said, "Dad, let me tell you somethin', man. I listen to a lot of stuff you say. I do a lot of stuff you tell me to do. But I can't do this one. They shot at my babies! It's *on* with these guys."

"No. You have got to forgive them."

I said, "How can I forgive them? They shot at my babies!"

So he talked me through the whole forgiveness thing. When he finished, I said, "I can't do that. I have got to do the law of the land! Do the neighborhood thing! We are going to shoot each other on sight!"

He said, "No. Forgive them."

I could not understand that. But I took the time to consider it. Then I told myself, *Okay, I'll try that.* I started forgiving those guys when I prayed.

One night I am somewhere, and I encounter those guys and immediately I'm thinking, *It's on, man!* I reach for my 9mm Glock on my hip—then *Ahhh! Ahhh! Ahhh!* and I wake up in a cold sweat. It's a dream. My heart is pounding. I am breathing real hard. It seemed so real. That was because God was telling me something: *You are only forgiving them with your mouth. Now forgive them from your heart.* So I kept up the praying.

Then one day I am in a store and those guys walk in. This is no dream. I think, *Man, I left my gun in the car.* But I just look at them, and I say, "How ya doin'?" They say, "Good. How you doin'?" That's it! They go about their business, and I go about mine. I think, *This ain't right. We were gonna get down, on sight!*

God was showing me, *See. You forgave from your heart.* Then I read in Proverbs 16 where it says, "When a man's ways are pleasing to the Lord, he makes even his enemies live at peace with him." God does that. When I saw those guys in that store, there was no friction, no animosity, no nothin' there. Just, "How ya doin'?" and it was done. I couldn't believe I could forgive them from my heart.

God will have you dealing with people that put a bad taste in your mouth, people that you don't go for. But you've got to be caught loving them. That was hard for me to accept. I look back at when I was in the gangs. It was so important for me to forgive, even those that were shooting at me, in order for me to walk with God. God says, *Do it my way. Then I got your back.*

Hill and Lewis

You will live in constant suspense, filled with dread both night and day, never sure of your life. In the morning you will say, "If only it were evening!" and in the evening, "If only it were morning!"

Deuteronomy 28

[Hunter often visits Calicinto Ranch—between Los Angeles and Palm Springs—operated by Henry Pirelli, his family and college-age camp counselors. The ranch hosts children and teens who have at least one parent in prison.]

Something happened between me and one of the counselors at the ranch. The ranch has this outside basketball court with bleachers down one side. About eighty kids were sitting there with the counselors, and I was standing on the basketball court getting ready to talk to them. Then I started speaking to the kids about how I grew up in the gangs, how God took me out of the gangs and made my life worth something. I told them about this one street in Long Beach called Lewis Avenue where we sold drugs, how we just closed off Lewis Avenue and took it for ourselves and how there were little kids on that street. I explained how we let the ice cream man drive his truck onto that street and then just took all his ice cream.

While I was talking I could see that this one counselor kept her hand over her mouth the whole time. I thought, *Mmm. What's wrong with her?* But I kept talking. I told them how on that street we would feed the little kids there, because we knew most of their parents were cracked-out.

When I finished, Mr. Pirelli came up to me and said, "August, you really got them. They are crying about how they want to forgive their mom and dad." Then that counselor came up to me. She said, "August, I remember you. I was one of those little kids. You guys gave us ice cream and barbeque. My dad ran with you. We lived on Hill and Lewis." I thought, *Wow! No wonder she put her hand over her mouth. She witnessed that.*

In my old neighborhood, Lewis Avenue was about two blocks long. On the south end it stopped at Hill Street. Going north, it dead-ended by some railroad tracks. There were apartment buildings all along Lewis Avenue, and on the east side of Lewis was an alley.

Our gang just closed off Lewis Avenue, right at Hill Street. That was our area: "Hill and Lewis." That's where I spent my time. My mom lived there, across the street from my sister. My friends were there. Snoop Dogg would hang out sometimes. Girls. Everybody. It was like a party there every day. It was mostly Rollin' 20's Crips, but the other gangs came through there. We would shoot dice together during the day, when it was neutral ground.

Every day, guys came through there with trucks. We would get boxes of lobster and shrimp and steaks, because those guys were on drugs. We had three or four barbeque grills going all the time, with our own chef. All the boosters brought all their hot items—clothes of all sizes, just masses of stuff—because this is where we sold all the drugs. This was headquarters.

But at night, Lewis Avenue was deadly. At night, there was gun play. At night, that street had violence. That's when the other gangs would try to creep up on you and do things. Scripture says that men love darkness, not light, because their deeds are evil. That's true.

We would be out on Lewis Avenue all night sellin' drugs. The street had a few lights, but it was dark. We would hang out in the "cut" between the apartment buildings, looking out from time to time to see if anybody was coming to buy drugs. No one could see us if they were out there looking down the street, because we were in the cut.

At night, the other gang would walk down the railroad tracks and then get in the alley to try to see where we were, to shoot at us. We knew they would be coming. One particular night, they came. One of the other gang members told me what happened later. In that gang there was one guy from down South. Oklahoma, I think. He was a square country boy when he moved to Long Beach. But then he got in that gang. He got tattoos all over his face and started smoking PCP. They had him just gone, man.

That night they were smoking that stuff. It was dark in the alley and they all had guns. We were in the cut, so they couldn't pinpoint us. They knew we had guns too, so they wanted to be careful. Somehow that kid from Oklahoma got separated from their group. Then he made a little noise in that alley and they all panicked—because they were paranoid from smokin' that PCP—and they shot him. *Boom-Boom-Boom!* When they saw that it was him, they left. They left him there and the cops came and shut down our street. We couldn't sell drugs for days.

That was everyday life on Hill and Lewis. That was normal stuff to us. It wasn't until I came into the knowledge of the truth that I knew that the life I was living was totally wrong, totally crazy.

I remember those kids on Lewis Avenue. We fed them. We gave them money. They looked up to us. When I was little, that's how I got sucked into the gangs. I needed love. The gangs accepted me. That was my love right there. That was my family. I was loyal to them.

So on Lewis Avenue, I could see things from the kids' perspective. Those kids were glamorized by the cars, the money, the clothes. But we were poisoning their minds, and our own mind being poisoned, we couldn't see that. I know that some of them made it out. One called me the other day.

That day at the ranch, that was a divine appointment. That counselor— her name is Jamika, and we became good friends. What she went through on Lewis Avenue, those kids in the bleachers were going through right then.

Back to New Orleans, again

...and a little child will lead them.

Isaiah 11

Eventually, things got to a point in the neighborhood where nothing was working for me. I couldn't sell drugs, the other gang was always shooting at me, the cops were pulling me over and jackin' me up, my homeboys were droppin' like flies all around me,... God was showing me, *Is this is what you choose, over me?* It was crazy!

It was strange too that around that time, my dad started calling me about once a month. The first time he asked me, "Hey, how are things goin'?" I said, "Aw, everything's goin' good." He said, "Are you sure?" and then he laughed and hung up. I thought, *That was a weird call.* He called me the second time and I told him things were getting a little tight, and he laughed again. By the next time he called, I could not even pay my rent; the money from drug-selling was just not there. Everything had dissolved. I told my dad, "It's really gettin' rough!" But he only laughed like before.

Then finally, one day he called me. He said, "How are things goin'?"

I said, "Dad, I'm in a corner. I can't do nothin'. I have no money. The police are jackin' me up! These guys are shootin' at me—"

"It's time now," he said.

"It's time now? For what?"

He said, "I've got your ticket ready."

"What ticket?"

He said, "You've got to come back down here to New Orleans and learn about the Lord."

So I flew back to New Orleans, because the cops and the gangsters were both trying to get me.

My dad was still pastor at his church in New Orleans, so I lived at his church. He would tell his people, "Now don't say nothin' to August. He'll hurt you! I got him!" I thought, *Why is this man telling these people that I will hurt them?* I started out as the janitor there. Before long, I was working all over that church.

New Orleans had these housing projects that were just full of young gangsters, and our church sat right in the midst of that. When I came down there, those gangsters recognized me as a gangster, because gangsters recognize other gangsters. We automatically connected. I was living in that church, but I still had a lot of street in me and those guys were drawn to me. They looked up to me as a gangster who was from California. They would come over to the church and I would tell them stories about what was happening in California and they would be amazed. We had a big gymnasium attached to the church, so I would have them playing basketball. My dad knew they were gangsters. He would say, "Man, this is cool. Just keep 'em comin'." So I kept the gymnasium full of gangsters.

My dad also had all these little boys in the church, because there were many single moms there that needed help raising their boys. Church was all they had. It was structure, and they needed that. New Orleans was the murder capital of the country at that time. I took time out for those little boys. I would take them to movies, the theme park—stuff like that. They loved me. They all slid up under me, because there was not a dad there.

At that time, I did not know how to read the Bible. I could not find my way from Exodus to Romans. So those little boys in the church started teaching me the Bible. I'd take my Bible and go to our worship service. The church would be full every Sunday morning, and—I'm telling you—every time I went in there, there was no other place to sit in that church except in the first pew up front, and those little guys were always right there waiting for me to sit down with them. There I was, a grown man, sitting in the front pew surrounded by those little guys.

During the worship service, when he was ready to preach, my dad would stand up front and call out a scripture verse so that the people there could open up their Bibles and find the verse and follow along with him. Whenever he did that, those little boys would get all excited to help me. "August, Ezekiel's back here! Right here! Look!" My dad would call out another verse and those boys would tell me, "No, August, no! Corinthians is up here!" They would show me where things were in the Bible. I was flabbergasted and embarrassed. I said to myself, *Man, these kids are teaching you. You should know this already*. I wanted to shrink. I would look behind me and the whole church would be watching these little guys teach me. My pride was wrecked!

But those little boys loved doing that. They were so happy that they could help me, they didn't pay attention to anything else. God has a way of working on us. I got over that pride. I humbled myself. I let those kids teach me, and I learned about the Lord.

Another thing that helped me learn at that time was that my dad was a hard driver. He drove everybody in that church. But I was as mean as a junkyard dog. I was tough. I listened to nobody! So God used my dad to drive me to learn. God knew that nobody else was qualified. I think of my dad at that time as King Nebuchadnezzar, a hard taskmaster. He drove me with everything he had. Even today, in my mind, I tell him, *Even if you never done nothin' for me in life, you drove me to Jesus. You blessed me right there.*

Even so, my relationship with my dad was kind of crazy. We would bump heads. Me and him ended up falling out. We had a falling out because of this deacon my dad had in his church. I knew the guy was a flim-flam man. He was manipulating the women in the church. But you could not tell my dad that, because he had groomed this guy. My dad told me he had a dream that I was causing division among the women in the church, and he pressed me on that; but it was that deacon. There was an uproar in the church, and somehow my name got mixed up in it. It was a mess, and I was tired of mess. My dad told me, "I don't trust you." I said, "You know what Dad? You have said a lot of stuff while I've been here. Now you don't trust me. I am not accepting that. There's no need for me to be here," and that made him mad, so I left. My cousin, who was his nephew, took me to the airport. I left New Orleans and went right back into my neighborhood. I had been in New Orleans about three or four years, from 1992 to 1996.

My dad and I didn't talk for a few years. He finally called me. He said, "Son. I wanna say I'm sorry."

"For what?"

"Things came to a head down here."

"Oh yeah?"

He said, "That deacon really *was* doin' that stuff."

"I tried to tell you."

"Yeah. He messed up my church and ran off with a lot of my people."

Those little boys that taught me the Bible, they suffered when that church split up. As long as they were at that church, things were good for them. But their moms left the church because of the way my dad was operating. I know that was the worst thing for those boys, because of the nature of that neighborhood. They didn't stand a chance. When I went down there last summer for my dad's funeral, I saw those boys' moms. They told me that one of those boys had got shot up real bad. Another had got killed. And one is in jail. They got older, you know?

Chapter 4 Study Guide

Return visit

A change of scene can help us. We can put behind old patterns of behavior which have enslaved us. If we leave our old power base, we can learn new lessons. We can humble ourselves and gain from new experiences. We might also find that our own past experiences are valuable to our new friends and acquaintances. Moving into a new situation might be just what God has planned for us. Are you due for a change of scene? Could you grow by leaving a familiar environment behind?

Tick Tock

Sometimes challenges seem too big for us. We feel ill-equipped. We feel alone. We get scared because of the "Goliath" or "Sasquatch" in front of us. But the Biblical view is that we are not to be afraid of such challenges. We are to know that God will give us the strength to fight the battle, as He did with David. God provides, protects and accompanies us as we face such challenges. When have you looked back over your life to see God's provisions for you in a difficult time? In what form did His love arrive?

My dog Noodles

We can think of our own need for protection as a little puppy. But that puppy can grow into a big dog that is "mean as the Devil." Healthy protection of our children can develop into oppression. Self-preservation can develop into false pride. Thrift can turn into greed. We can be overly-protective of our plans and goals to the point that we miss the important thing that God has in store for us. Protection may be justified at the start of many things. But without periodic reassessment, we can lose our perspective and start protecting the wrong thing, the wrong way. What do you spend your time and energy safeguarding? What "dog" do you have at the end of your emotional leash as you relate to others? Is it a dog like Noodles or a dog like Brownie in Chapter 1?

The fish market

Is your world broad or narrow? If you are opinionated, judgmental and prideful, your world will shrink. If you are accepting, curious and welcoming, your world will expand. Jesus associated with tax collectors, prostitutes and the sick. The religious leaders of Jesus' day, even Jesus' family, feared what was new. We can be realistic and discerning about someone's circumstances without being judgmental. Do you judge others without exercising discernment? Have you ever been misjudged by people?

Violated

We all have boundaries around ourselves, to keep us safe. Your intellectual boundary tells you when someone is forcing their ideas on you; your physical boundary tells you when someone is moving in too close to you; your spiritual boundary protects your deepest beliefs; your financial boundary keeps people from misusing your hard earned money; your emotional boundary guards you from manipulation and protects your feelings; and legal boundaries protect our freedoms.

There are people who do not respect boundaries. They cross over too easily. Sometimes people in authority fail to respect those boundaries—doctors, attorneys, police officers or a spouse. When those people violate us, it can be especially damaging. Who has violated one of your boundaries? Which boundary is hardest for you to safeguard in your own life—emotional, physical, intellectual, spiritual, financial?

Making peace

You can get revenge under the "the rules of the penitentiary." But revenge will never give you satisfaction. You might feel that temporarily, but you will eventually look back at your behavior with regret. When feeling revengeful, it is an especially good time to trust God. If you have ever wanted revenge but then dropped the idea, what did you replace the feeling with? How did you deal with the harm that was originally done to you?

"Little Dog"

Guilt serves a purpose. It calls us back to important internal standards that we should uphold. If we violate those standards, guilt is God's loving way of redirecting us back again. If we don't follow God's direction, guilt makes our mind and feelings circle back to what is wrong, not so that we are stuck with the guilt, but so that we relearn and recommit to what God wants for us. If you have good character, guilt won't let you go until there is some resolution. We should be grateful for that. If you have felt legitimate guilt, what allowed you to release it? How did you grow in the process?

My mom's ride by

If we lead a dangerous lifestyle, someone else can get hurt. While most of us are not involved in violent gangs, many of us are involved in personal situations that are dangerous to us—and others—emotionally. The results can be distressing. Has some decision for your own life negatively impacted loved ones close to you? Describe the emotional environment you have created around yourself. Is it healthy for others?

How ya doin'?

As individual human beings operating on our own, we have very little power to do anything but the "neighborhood thing." We react in obvious human ways to people who hurt us. But when we look at the world through God's eyes, we have a chance of loving our worst enemies and of overcoming our strongest destructive impulses. What happened the last time you reacted impulsively when someone hurt you? Have you had experiences where, in resolving conflict, you did things God's way? What was the result?

Hill and Lewis

Our families are where we learn. There we learn about personal freedom, relating to people, structuring time, who we are as a person and power in this world. In a family we can learn about the good in life—about boundaries, closeness, enjoyment, productivity, personal value, that God is in charge and that He lets us co-create with Him. Or, in families we can learn the bad—about physical and emotional violence, manipulation, neglect, disorganization and worthlessness. Which people and experiences in your growing up moved you in the direction of goodness in life? Which people and experiences in your growing up moved you in the direction of the bad things in life?

Back to New Orleans, again

God is always at work in the ups and downs in our lives. Things will be going along fine, and then begin to shut down, dry up, or even turn bad. Then we wonder where God is. We feel lost, confused and resentful.

God allows us to go through ups and downs to create growth and appreciation for life. After a down time, you are energized to move forward. You want to shake off the pain you have been through. You are ready and eager to move forward. Then God can use you, and you have learned about yourself, life, or others. If we resist the ups and downs that God gives us, we get stuck. The ups and downs can be scary, but less so when we remember that God is in charge. When we remember that, the ride can be exhilarating. Are you skilled at recognizing the down times that God may send you? What have you learned from the ups and downs in your life?

Chapter 5 – Portland

Elmo

I remember one of August's buddies here in Long Beach that he tried to keep under control—Elmo. Elmo always drove some old Cadillac, and he might drive that Cadillac down the street backwards at forty miles an hour. And shootouts! Elmo wanted a shootout every day. He would take his gun and shoot out of his car window. And if you thought you were the top shooter in the neighborhood, Elmo would visit you and it would be Gunsmoke!

People were scared of Elmo. He was a short, stocky guy with a big ol' head and little bitty teeth in his mouth. And he could smell fear. If he smelled your fear, he was on you like a chicken hawk with a pistol in his pocket. That's how he was. That's how he lived.

Elmo was a good dude, and we liked him. But when he got all that prison time, there was a sigh of relief in the neighborhood. People were happy he was gone.

Younger brother Jason

When I left New Orleans, I got entangled back in Long Beach with one of my old homeboys named Elmo. Elmo was a piece of work. Every time I would see that guy, he would automatically make me laugh. Elmo would ask me, "Why you always laughin' at me?" I'd say, "Aw Elmo, I don't know." He'd say, "Well you better stop that, or we'll get out the pistols!" I'd say, "Elmo, I'll beat you down before you get out your pistol." Right now Elmo is in one of the penitentiaries here in California. Elmo ain't never comin' home.

Elmo was a robber—always kept a gun on him. He loved to rob establishments—and people. I would tell Elmo, "You better slow down boy, or they're gonna lock you up for good." He'd say, "They'll have to catch me first."

One time Elmo and I are sitting in a car in front of this restaurant. The actual restaurant is on the first floor, but upstairs is the office for the restaurant. We are in the parking lot, talking. Elmo gets out and says, "I gotta use the restroom," and he goes inside that restaurant. But he takes a long time. I get out of the car to talk to someone on the pay phone that's right there by the restaurant, and while I'm on the phone, I look up to the second floor and I can see Elmo with his back to the window and people standing there with their hands up in the air. I think, *Man!* Then Elmo comes running out yelling, "Come on! Let's go! Let's go!" I say, "Man, what'd you do?" He just robbed that place! Later we got into it. I told him, "Man, don't *ever* put me in a place like *that*." We split up about that, but we were still friends.

After a while there was word goin' around that Elmo was robbing everything in the neighborhood. So I got together with Elmo and told him, "Man, your name is in the street. You need to slow down." But he had got with a group of women and these women had pumped up his head and told him that he was Robin Hood and he can go ahead and rob the rich and bring it all to them because they were poor, you know? So this is what he was doing. You see, Elmo was the type of guy that always wanted a girl. But when he got one, they would use him, because Elmo was,… Well, Elmo wasn't the most handsomest-lookin' guy, you know what I'm saying? And so Elmo—oh boy, I loved that boy like a brother—he said to me, "Aw man, you're just jealous 'cause all the women are lookin' at me now." I said, "Elmo, they don't care nothin' about you! They want the money that you're gettin'! They don't care if you go to jail right now! You'd never see any one of those girls again if you did." But he wouldn't listen.

Then I heard that Elmo robbed an insurance place and they had this guy there that was a pastor from Africa, and when Elmo was robbing this guy he tried to grab the gun and the gun went off and shot the guy in the chest and killed him. When I heard that, I thought, *Aw, Elmo.* Elmo got something like four hundred years, plus a life sentence.

God got me out of that mess I had with Elmo. When Elmo went to prison, I thought, *I'm gettin' out of here.* I went up to Portland, Oregon. That's where I ended up.

Portland

> *Now listen, you who say, "Today or tomorrow we will go to this or that city, spend a year there, carry on business and make money." Why, you do not even know what will happen tomorrow. What is your life? You are a mist that appears for a little while and then vanishes.*

James 4

I knew this one homeboy from the Rollin' 20's Crips. We had made money together selling drugs. By 1997, he was in Portland and he was having trouble with the Bloods there. So he called me to come up to Portland to check a few of those guys for him. He said we would do the work, he would pay me and then he would take me back to the airport.

After I got to Portland, I sent for some of my boys from Long Beach, to come and help me check those Bloods. We sent them airline tickets. When they got there, I had everything set up and we dealt with those Bloods.

When we got finished with those Bloods there in Portland, my homeboy said to me, "Let me drive your boys to the airport," and we put them on a plane back to Long Beach.

Then he says to me, "Okay. Now, when are you leavin'?"

I say, "Um, tomorrow."

"Well, I paid you your money."

I say, "Yeah. But I'm here now."

"No! No! No! You can't come here and take over! That was our deal! You were gonna leave as soon as everything's done!"

I say, "Now, hold on buddy. I'm just gonna check out the town, to see if
I—"

"Naw, naw, naw!" and he shook his head.

I said, "Well, I know you don't mind me hangin' around your little town
for a while." He got so mad.

I came to realize that Portland was nice and slow. I said to myself, *This is
Mayberry and I'm Andy Griffith*. It was just what I was looking for. I told my
homeboy, "My mind is made up. I'm hangin' out here." So I just took over
the little thing that my homeboy had going there. The gangsters that he had
me check became my best friends, and I had the green light to do whatever I
wanted.

But in reality, my life in Portland was a mess. I was smokin' marijuana
and sellin' ounces of cocaine. I kept a 9mm Glock on me, and I was in the
midst of the whole business of selling drugs there in Portland.

So God really started dealing with me. I had a void in me, an emptiness.
And I could not fill it no matter what I did on the streets. I was looking for a
way to fill that void.

I found out that to fill that void I had to go to church. I would hang out
with the gangsters and sell drugs all week long, and then go to church on
Sunday. The gangsters thought I was crazy. They'd say, "Look at him! He
hangs out all week with us—drinkin', smokin', sellin' drugs—and then on
Sunday morning he's gonna get up and go to church." They knew that about
me.

I bought my first Bible for fifty-seven dollars, a *Thomson-Chain King James
Study Bible*, which I have on my bed board to this day; I still do my morning
devotions from that Bible. I was attending this one church in Portland, to
hear what the preacher had to say. I didn't understand it all, but I knew it was
true. I could keep up with him in my Bible whenever he called out a verse.
And I listened to him, to fill that void.

I wanted to get right with God. But still, I would come out of that church and my cell phone would ring and I would meet someone there in the church parking lot to sell them an ounce of cocaine. I was making so much money! Then I heard the preacher when he taught out of the third chapter of Malachi about paying tithes, about bringing tithes into the storehouse. So I wanted to pay my ten percent, and I started to do that. One time my sister Delreece was in church sitting next to me, because she was staying with me. She put two dollars in the collection plate and she saw me put in five hundred. She whispered, "Are you crazy?" Later she phoned my family, "He done lost his mind! He's givin' all this money to the church!" But I had learned about tithes, and I knew what kind of money I was making. My sister didn't understand what I was going through.

I would catch myself reading the Bible at night. And every morning I would get up and make some coffee and roll me up a big ol' stogie of marijuana and sit down and read the Bible. It was crazy, because I didn't know what I was reading. But I had to fill that void.

A lot of times I just cried. It got to the point where I could not sleep at night. Then one morning, I just cried out—*Ahhhhhhhhh!* I busted all the blood vessels in my eyes and my nose was snottin' up. I just cried out to God.

Then God gave me this verse from Proverbs: "Trust in the LORD with all your heart and lean not on your own understanding; in all your ways acknowledge him, and he will make your paths straight." God was speaking to me through that verse. See, I was thinking wrong. I thought I had to change my ways *before* I could acknowledge God. But I realized, this verse was talking about all my ways *then and there*—my low-down ways, my weed-smokin' ways, my cocaine-sellin' ways, my drinkin' ways, my foul-mouth ways. God was telling me that I don't need to wait to get myself together to acknowledge Him. I could acknowledge Him in my present ways.

And I was already doing that! When I was sellin' drugs and then would go to the church, I was acknowledging God. When I was smokin' marijuana while trying to read the Bible, I was acknowledging Him. I thought, *This is what He means! I can acknowledge Him even in my ways that I cannot control.*

So God delivered me. He had me stop selling drugs, He had me stop smoking weed, He had me stop drinking liquor—all at once. He told me to leave all that stuff and get out of Portland and go back to Long Beach, to a little church where my kids were going. It was their cousin's church. His name was Chester.

Stress, peace and focus

> *And the peace of God, which passes all understanding, shall keep your hearts and minds through Christ Jesus.*
>
> *Philippians 4*
>
> *God did this so that men would seek him and perhaps reach out for him and find him, though he is not far from each one of us. For in him we live and move and have our being.*
>
> *Acts 17*

God does not want us operating out of stress. That stuff will kill you. Our bodies are not designed to be stressed out, to be overwhelmed, to be fretting. That's why the Bible says, "Cast all your anxiety on him." God is saying, "Look. You cannot handle things. Give them to me. Let me handle them."

We can face a storm in our life. That storm can bring persecution, it can bring tribulation, it can bring a battle. When we face a storm, we tend to run, because we don't want to deal with things. We want things easy. We want things always to be good. But God allows the storm. It is through the storm that God builds character in us, that God strengthens us, that God moves us up to the next level. I face storms one after another. I accept them. I think, *Okay Lord. Here's another one*, because in Him, I live, move and have my being.

We should embrace trials and tribulations and persecution. God is building character, God is strengthening you, God is using that to mature you.

I will sometimes have trouble and I don't see a light at the end of the tunnel. But I've got no business gettin' stressed out, no business worryin', no business frettin'! I give it to God. He keeps me in perfect peace. You only get perfect peace from Him. We don't even understand that peace. It surpasses all understanding. That's because it is perfect peace.

We need that peace in the circumstances of our lives. That peace is there so that we can maintain our integrity, our character, our accountability—just *maintain* as a man of God, no matter how much pressure there is. I'm so glad that God knows my situation better than I do. I just enjoy myself.

A lot of hard stuff is going to happen around you. Don't let that make you fret. Don't let that get you out of your character. Don't let that weaken your faith. Because when you stand on your faith, you operate out of the character that God has instilled in you. When I face trouble, people tell me, "Man, you need to do *this*, you need to do *that*." I tell them, "Man, I am not doin' *nothin'* but sit right here and let God do His thing."

Never let a situation dictate policy to you. God schooled me on that a long time ago. If you face trouble, you need to be the same person you are when things are going good. That trouble should not dictate how you act and operate. Instead, *love* is dictating how you act and operate. And even when we are faced with a situation that is overwhelming—I mean, that is just crazy— we still operate on the character that God instilled in us. We are not letting that trouble tell us how we should operate, how we should look, what we should do. God would have you stand on your faith. If you have faith, no situation will dictate policy to you. You are giving God room enough to work in your life, because you are not trying to do it.

Some days there's so much confusion whirling around in my head, it makes me feel like screaming, "Stop!" But by me being rooted and grounded in Christ, I am able to withstand it. I stick to, I practice, I operate out of that scripture, "Cast your anxiety on Him."

God—*man!*—He is working out of precision, He is hitting every area, He is right on target. Our job is to focus on Him. But for Him, everything is like clockwork. He is steady at working things out. I'm excited to listen to God, and to watch what He does. And I am able to sleep without worry in my heart. I lay down at night and love to sleep.

Chester's church

So I left Portland and went back to Long Beach. And look at how God works! He told me to take my tithe, which was about five hundred dollars, and put it in an envelope and take it with me when I went to Long Beach. As soon as I got back to Long Beach, I went to this little church called Open Doors of Faith. It was my kids' mom's cousin's church, and his name was Chester.

I knew Chester from when we ran in the streets, and that first Sunday morning I went there he was excited to see me. He had been pastoring there for years, together with his wife. At the time, I did not know what was going on in Chester's church, but I am there that day, and I hand him that envelope.

I say, "Here's my tithe."

Chester says, "Well, thank you August."

"—for you and your wife."

"Aw, praise the Lord brother." Then he says "August, will you say something to the church?"

At that time, I am shy about public speaking, so I say, "Naw, naw, Pastor."

"Please. Share something with us."

So after a while, Chester has me stand up and he introduces me to his people sitting there in the pews, hands me the microphone and then sits down next to his wife. I am shell-shocked standing up there. I feel like I have a bomb in my hand that is ready to explode any minute now.

I think, *What can I say?*

The Lord tells me, *Speak about tithes.*

Okay. I lift that microphone and I say, "You know, pay your tithes. Bring your ten percent into the storehouse. God will bless you."

When I say that, Chester jumps up out of his chair and grabs that microphone from me and starts speaking to me and the people there. He says, "Man! Ain't nobody but the *Lord* sent you here today to speak on that, because you don't know what is happenin' in this church! Man! I've been fightin' with these people in this church about payin' tithes and they've been comin' against me sayin' that I'm takin' the tithes and buyin' my wife dresses and not spendin' the money on the church, and I have been *fightin'* and *fightin'* with these people, tryin' to get them to understand that it's right that they pay tithes!" I'm looking at Chester while he is speaking and I think, *Wow! I didn't know that all this was goin' on.*

Then Pastor Chester keeps going. "I just told my wife this morning that this was gonna be my last sermon, that I was not preachin' no more, that I was givin' up! I told her that I wasn't gonna deal with these people no more! I wasn't gonna fight with them no more! Man, I am just *tired!*" Then Chester turns to me and says, "But August, I know the Lord sent you here today to encourage me, because this was gonna be my last Sunday." I looked at Chester, and I was amazed!

That's why it is so important that we obey God. When God tells you to do something, do it. Obey Him. Do it, because there is a whole big picture behind what you think you already know. There's a whole lot more that you don't understand. Just say, *Yes, Lord.* I didn't know all that was going on at

Chester's church. Chester was planning to give up his church. He wasn't going to preach anymore. But I was able to encourage him by coming there and speaking on tithes.

That blew me away. And it made me look at Abraham, because of Abraham's obedience to God when God told him, *Get up and get to a land you no nothing about. I'm going to bless you.* I thank God that Abraham obeyed, because here we are, Abraham's offspring in the faith, but only because Abraham obeyed God way back then. If you don't obey God, you rob yourself of the blessings that God has for you. You will never know the plan that God has for your life.

This all happened right before my brother Eldridge died. He was suffering from cirrhosis of the liver and I started to take him to church with me. I became the first deacon in that church.

Then the praise and worship team quit at that church, and God told me, *Get up and do praise and worship.* I said, *Lord, I can't sing.* He said, *Do praise and worship.* So I would wake up on Sundays and get to church early and meet with Chester's wife and do the praise and worship at the church. I started lovin' doin' it.

Then the Sunday School teacher left. The Lord said, *Do the Sunday School.* I said, *Lord, I'm not a teacher.* He said, *Do the Sunday School.* So I become the Sunday School teacher.

I was doing that, and then the guy that did the maintenance and the cleaning and the painting around the church—he left the church. The Lord said, *You step up to the plate.* So I became the maintenance man at the church. I was the everything-man at that church.

Another friend that I knew from early on in the gangs, Pastor Glenn, he would come over and visit Chester's church. He'd say, "Boy, Pastor Chester. God has blessed you with a faithful deacon. Every time I come here, August is taking care of this church." Glenn knew what that meant in my life, because I grew up with Glenn.

I was faithful at Chester's church. I stayed at that church for quite a while. God was getting me ready to go on the journey that I am on now. If at any time I was disobedient, I would have never got to where I am now.

A beautiful day in the neighborhood

Contribution by Dean Schiffman
January 17, 2009—Long Beach, California

As August Hunter and I stood at the curb on a chilly Saturday morning in January, Martin L. King Avenue appeared nicely broad and properly paved, with freshly-painted traffic lines. The straightness of the Avenue as it cut through central Long Beach allowed me to see far in both directions. That day's Martin Luther King Day Parade would begin just blocks away on my left, and finish way to my right at—yes—Martin Luther King Park. Hunter and I were there to watch the parade from the stoop of the Love Unlimited Community Church—Glenn E. Lassiter, Pastor—and to interview Lassiter afterward, for this book.

As I watched, long white sawhorses were being placed across the streets that intersected the Avenue. A few official vehicles had begun their back-and-forth patrol of the parade route. Lassiter's church—a boxy two-story structure painted white with blood-red trim—is only twenty feet from the Avenue, and his parishioners began to join us soon after we positioned our folding chairs on the top step of its gray-carpeted stoop. An appreciative congregant in his seventies shared the bag of deep-fried apple fritters I had purchased at the doughnut shop across the Avenue, although his wife gave me a stern look.

Much can be seen from that stoop. To the left, just down the Avenue, is a nifty little hand-wash carwash operated, as it turns out, by Willie McGinist's uncle, McGinist a Cleveland Brown. Directly across the Avenue from the stoop, behind a block-long chain link fence, is Gwynn Field and Long Beach Polytechnic High School, where McGinist and big leaguer Tony Gwynn played their high school ball (as have numerous notable professional sports figures, past and present). Looking a little right from there is the doughnut shop, and then Pacific Coast Highway as it cuts across the Avenue; Hunter had described for me how during the Rodney King riots in 1992, the liquor store on that corner was defended from the roof with automatic weapons. Just to the right of the church stoop is a tidy corner mall with the Pee & Gee Fish Market, VIP Records where Snoop Dogg got his start, and a local barbeque place whose people were preparing for the parade crowd.

I sat and watched, as the time for the parade grew closer. A tall White man in a dark suit walked hurriedly down the Avenue toward the parade assembly area. A street vender strode by several times pulling a red wagon stocked with foot-long pink-plastic party horns, holding one of them to his lips repeatedly, to blast it at the assembling crowd. Bicycles were finding their way through the sawhorses. Two thin women dressed in t-shirts, blue jeans and flip-flops peddled their wide-tire beach cruisers steadily down the Avenue toward us. As they glided past the church, they turned their ghostly-white faces to look at us, and I guessed from their same-blonde hair and blank stares that they were a mother-daughter crystal meth team on wheels. Hunter pointed to a cluster of ATV quads—each with its white-helmeted rider—that was forming on Pacific Coast Highway near the liquor store, which, he explained, meant the Police Gang Task Force was now in place.

With the air warming wonderfully and the parishioners of the Love Unlimited Community Church now boiling an oversized pot of water for their makeshift hotdog stand, I knew the parade was beginning. The first to come was a line of local politicians, each waving from the back of a new Mustang convertible, including the tall man in the dark suit. Then began two hours of delightful human spectacle. Mixed up in no particular sequence were orderly military bands, vans and flatbed trucks laden with raucous congregants broadcasting Jesus from loudspeakers, and high-whining hordes of Japanese motorcycles. I was repeatedly dazzled by the rows and rows of young girls marching before blaring brass bands, their faces beautiful and nobly determined, high-stepping to the drum beat, twirling large flags unfurled for the day, all of them sparkling in their sun-struck sequined costumes. A serious-looking Black man with a shaved head and full beard gripped the steering wheel of his Pontiac Bonneville lowrider, painted the same yellow as the stripes on the pavement only shockingly more shiny. He swerved and jerked his way down the Avenue, the hydraulics of his lowrider hissing and banging as he went.

Both Hunter and Lassiter became animated when they spotted a vintage 1970s Dodge Coronet coming into view, classic in its black-and-white four-door design. It carried Police Chief Batts on the passenger side as he gently and continuously waved his right hand, positioned out the open passenger-side window, just above the *Long Beach Police* emblem on the door. Pastor Glenn tried to keep half a hotdog balanced on his paper plate as he yelled excitedly to Hunter about how, "that guy got that thing out of the garage to start chasing us again!" to which Hunter responded, "Aw man, that thing brings back memories."

Dancing would erupt as the parade passed. Still holding her cell phone, a tall broad-shouldered woman in a red feed cap and brown knit pants leaped from the crowd, stepped into the midst of a passing jazz band and danced beautifully nose-to-nose with an awesome character dressed like Big Bird, only Mardi Gras style. But my favorite came later, with the passing of *Tamborazo Banda—Galeana de Michoacan*. First came a cherry-red Ford pickup truck hauling a full drum set and its teenage virtuoso. His partner, positioned opposite him in the truck bed, seemed to have been assigned exclusively to the base drum, which he beat energetically with a long green-tufted stick. Behind the truck walked a brass band of eight or so teenage boys dressed in street clothes, whose masterful tuba player anchored their rousing Latin beat. A handsome lone dancer in his 20s followed just behind. Medium height and well-groomed, he wore a blue long-sleeve dress shirt, and black loose-fitting denims which were held up by a fancy white belt and were—at the bottom—pulled over the shafts of his tan cowboy boots. The dancer's right forearm was positioned in front of the belt, while his left arm was lifted as if giving a pledge. Clearly his imaginary dance partner was satisfactorily following the intricate movements of his cowboy boots, because he stared dreamily into her eyes. He was continuously executing some Latin-based dance step which I am not qualified to name and whose rhythms were accentuated with each manly blast from the tuba. It was all too much for a brown-haired girl sitting on the curb. She sprang up, strode over near the young man, and gracefully replaced his imaginary dance partner. I do not think the young man noticed, although his dreamy look became dreamier. The girl's tight shorts and bare legs revealed an equal command of the dance step, and she knew that her unprotected feet were entirely safe from the smooth but vigorous action of the cowboy boots against the asphalt. The two so communed for a few minutes, creeping along behind the Ford. The whole incident seemed joyously steamy, although I am not sure what the ladies at the Love Unlimited Community Church thought.

Old friends stopped to chat with Hunter, most of them aging former gangsters; I could hear the news updates, mostly bad. Hunter spotted one of them walking along the Avenue, shouted to have him stop and talk, but got no response. It seemed to sadden Hunter. "He don't even recognize me," I heard him say. It may have been Hunter's blue *Prison Chaplain* baseball cap that obscured his identity.

When the parade ended, a massive white street-sweeping machine rolled briskly along the curb, *hishing-hishing-hishing* and honking angrily at vehicles parked in its way. After a long interview with Lassiter, Hunter and I drove down to King's Park for the post-parade festivities. There I met Hunter's stylish sister Fabiola and three of her friends. At one end of the park, the local churches were featuring their gospel choirs under a large tent. Hunter drew my attention to the other end, where there were game booths and party jumpers. "See that area there? That's thick with young gangsters," he explained. "They're all makin' plans for tonight." We got hungry and bought ourselves double-bacon cheeseburgers, and I drove Hunter's SUV back to San Diego as he napped in the passenger seat to get ready for his Sunday sermon at Donovan Prison.

Hunter called me at six o'clock the next morning. He himself had already gotten a phone call. Overnight, a guy he knew had gunned down two young men who were breaking into his house. "They're dead," Hunter told me. "Probably some of those guys we saw in the park."

Pastor Glenn and the Love Unlimited Community Church

> *I met Glenn in the gangs, when we were youngsters. He was the littlest guy in the gang, but he ended up using the most drugs. Once I asked him, "Little Lass, are you gonna make it through all this? I hope so." Later, during my transformation, Glenn was always next to me. When God dealt with me, Glenn helped me through it all.*
>
> *August Hunter*

[Pastor Glenn E. Lassiter gave this interview after he, Hunter and I watched the 2009 Long Beach Martin Luther King Day Parade from the steps of Lassiter's church.]

My dad could always vividly recall the scene when, as a young boy, he accidentally shot and killed his baby sister. His father forgave him. But my dad's mother sent him away to live with her parents, near a little town called Percellville, in Virginia. His mom's younger brothers, who made bootleg liquor, were there too. As he grew up, my dad began to drink, and his parents' marriage broke up back home.

When I was thirty years old—my dad was dead by then—I traveled to Virginia, met my dad's family for the first time and did some research. I got their accounts of what happened to my dad's baby sister and to his mom. I gathered the information, pulled it all together and pieced together the full story. Then I told the story back to my dad's older cousins, who were by then these ladies in their seventies. They agreed that the information which I had gathered and how I had analyzed it was correct and in its context.

In his late teens, my dad went into the Air Force, and then married my mom. I was born in 1960 at Fort Dix, New Jersey—their fourth child. When I was three, my dad resigned from the Air Force. He got the idea to move from New Jersey back to Virginia. But my mom had her mother, a brother and a slew of uncles back here on the West Coast. So one day, five of us children and my dad and my mom—who was six months pregnant—got into our new Chevrolet station wagon to drive down Interstate 95 to Virginia. But the first night, with my mom driving and my dad in the front seat in a drunken stupor, we detoured west for a three-day trip. My mom hauled that Chevy station wagon as fast as she could across the country, to get her family to California. She kept feeding my dad more booze whenever he started waking up. After she drove far enough, my dad woke up in Barstow, California. He had never seen I-40 or I-15 before, and he was smokin' hot that she drove his car all the way to California. That was around January 1963, because my sister was born that February. We moved to *this* neighborhood in Long Beach in 1964.

My dad was a functioning alcoholic. He owned two homes and had money in the bank. After a series of detox programs, his drinking remained. He was trying to drown things out, to forget them. His marriage to my mom ended in 1970. He remarried in 1973 and died in 1974 at the tender age of forty-four. I was fourteen. We were close.

Here, in the inner city, you will find broken families, single moms, welfare,... And there's indigents. There's poverty. Those things bring about the desperate need to be accepted. Acceptance—the lust for acceptance—is what can draw kids into trouble. When there is turmoil at home—you look for love, you look for acceptance, you look for approval, outside of the home. You go to the streets. That leads to crime, jail and death—premature death as we understand it.

Until my mid-teens, I played sports—Pop Warner Football and track—and was considered to be the most sports-analytical person in the neighborhood. I had all these sports stats in my brain. Everybody would get a kick out of me mimicking Howard Cosell. I hoped to some day be a sports commentator.

I had those aspirations, but the streets of the inner city have a way of calling you. When I was thirteen, an older peer introduced me to marijuana. At fourteen that escalated into Angel Dust, although I was still functioning in sports and school. By my late-teens, I was a regular user of PCP—and marijuana and beer and sometimes hard alcohol and sometimes uppers and sometimes downers. I had a friend whose older brother was a full-fledged dope dealer. We could get all the cocaine and dope we wanted. We took it, we used it, and we tried to sell portions of it. I lost my focus on sports and school, and started hustling to survive. No matter what your aspirations are, at that point you begin to understand, you begin to accept, you begin to believe that the inner city is what you are. You become part of its fabric. You form pacts with people and gangs and coalitions of gangs. And that's how I met August. He had come to California from New Orleans, and I learned from him that New Orleans was just as ruthless in its makeup as Long Beach or LA.

I had a drug overdose at age sixteen. That evening I had concluded that I was going home early—no nightlife. But then a friend came by and said, "I got my sister's car," and another friend was with him whose mother was a pharmacist. So that night, there were five of us in a car full of drugs, and I could use all I wanted.

Although I was the littlest guy in the group, that night I snorted big time. But at one point, my body went stiff and cold. My friends decided to drop me off at another friend's house. I stayed there until my high came down. Then I went home and carried on as usual. But my mother knew that I was out all night, which was not common.

After a while, the doctors found out that I had heart problems, and I had to tell my mother what happened. She said, "You're in sports. What's wrong?" The doctors got a handle on things and my heart came back, although in a matter of months I was back on drugs. I was managing school, but the street life was dominating me.

After high school I joined the U.S. Navy. But with my desire for drugs, that ended. I thank God for my honorable discharge. I came back to Long Beach.

In 1979 I saw a girl I had met in middle school through my sister. I remembered her. Her name was Joyce. My interest heightened. I was determined, and I maneuvered my way into her life. I put the drugs on hold, because this was a clean-cut girl. But after I secured the relationship, I delved back into drugs—strongly—without her knowing, for two years. I stayed away from her when I did drugs and I was always very respectful of her parents. The things my dad had taught me were coming back to work to my advantage.

After two years, there was this new system of drug use—freebasing cocaine. I didn't know what it was and I was happy with PCP. But one night a gentleman, a school teacher, introduced me to freebasing.

That would have been 1981, because that spring I have another overdose. It is unlike the first one. I am aware that my heart is beating fast in my chest, that I am perspiring profusely, that I am about to die. I tell my siblings that something is wrong but they think I am fooling around so I drive myself rapidly to Long Beach Memorial Hospital to get a particular type of drug that slows the heart back down. They offer me drug treatment, which I do not pursue.

A month later I am back using cocaine. Then I lose a good job. My hustling days are over, because, as I know, that leads to prison. I exhaust my bank account, and my sweet-hearted girlfriend is saying, "You *have* to get it together. Now I *know* that you use drugs. I can see it." That fall I was arrested for a DUI, even though at the time I was on PCP.

In December of 1981, Joyce invited me to this little church, to a "Watch Meeting" where the congregants get together to thank God and watch-in the New Year. I told her I would come, but my intention on New Year's Eve was to party and get high.

On New Year's Eve, the party somehow ends early and I am at home in my room, thinking. For two months I have been soaking in depression. Now another year is coming in and my life is nothing like I thought it would be. I am still a dope addict. I am still a loser. There is nothing to involve me in journalism, or sports, or broadcasting. My Navy career ended in failure, and everything else around me is crumbling. Nobody in my family can help me, and the best relationship I ever had with a girl is about to go away. I consider suicide. But at eleven-thirty that Thursday night, I get up and go to the Watch Meeting. I come through the door high. The people receive me warmly and pray for me. My high comes down.

For the next three days I have no desire for drugs, and that was unusual. On Sunday morning, January 3rd, something says to me, *Why don't you go back to that little church?* I have no church attire, no church savvy, no church lingo.

But I walk—in what attire I have—back to the little church and I give my life to the Lord. Today I am celebrating twenty-seven years of clean and sober living. The Lord blessed me.

In a few weeks I had a new hard-working job with low pay, but I was saving money. Six months after that January 3rd day, I preached my first sermon in a pulpit, there at that church. A month later I proposed to Joyce and at Thanksgiving time we were married, now for twenty-six years. Her parents were simple people from Louisiana and they welcomed me warmly into their family. That's where I am today. I am thankful for our three sons. Joyce is the best thing that God has brought in bodily form into my life.

For twenty-four years, the pastor at this church mentored me, with a forty-one year age difference between us. He taught me the Gospel and the Bible and how to behave myself as a gentleman and how to treat my wife and how to approach things in the inner city and the pitfalls to stay away from. Then he named me as his successor and passed away. I took over as pastor, not too long ago.

We are located in Long Beach District Six, which is dense with people who are impacted by poverty, crime and gangs. But there is a mystique about this area. People come together out of need. There is a bond between them that gives them hope. It provides a strange sort of safety net. The experiences of the inner city involve some shame, but I wouldn't trade them for anything.

Men come to this church after long stretches in prison, and back in the 70s we would have been from rival gangs. I embrace them and help them and guide them, and they are flabbergasted by that, because they only remember the 70s. I can say to them, "It will be alright. You'll make it. You don't have to go back to prison. The streets are what we came from, but that's not who we are."

I have watched the schools change. I have watched Martin Luther King Avenue change. City Council persons come and go, and mayors. But our churches have been steady—some for a hundred years—and the fabric of the community stays somewhat the same. I see young people that have the same issues I had thirty years ago, and I try to steer them just a little bit away from where they are going.

I am very serious about pastoral ministry. I am *serious!* I do not have time for people who play games with it, or politicize it. I have no energy for that. I know August feels the same way. There was no reason for God to let me live through that overdose in 1976. There was no reason for God to let me live through that overdose in 1981. No *human* reason. But God had a reason. I learned that my life could be used by God, that I could impact somebody else. The first twenty-one years of my life were mine. The rest belong to God. My hair is not jet black like it was when I became a Christian, but I still have a portion of my youth left. I am going to use every ounce of strength in me to help somebody.

When you are young, you hear about God and that we can't see Him. When I was a young teen, God pulled and tugged at me. But I resisted, because I was unfamiliar with His voice. Then I actually encountered Him, seeing that He really does change lives.

When I first met August in the gangs, we ran together daily. But our lives drifted apart, mine into drugs and his into status as a major Long Beach drug lord. Later, as I found my faith, August began to vacillate between the life of a drug lord and life in prison. In the 1990s, we reacquainted. I was able to encourage August in his new faith, when he was a deacon at a small church in West Long Beach. The pastor at that church was a guy I went to high school with. I would visit that church periodically and August would be there and we would have long talks. We naturally reconnected—no hustling, no games, no schemes. Just two men conversing about experiences, and August telling me that he was leaving that other life alone for good.

Chapter 5 Study Guide

Elmo

Earthly power can be attractive. It can also be destructive. If you know who you are—a child of God, made in His image—you will have enough power. Otherwise you will be tempted to get power by your position, by the people you know, by how scary you can make yourself or by how deceptive you are. But that type of power is never satisfying and is always tugging at you for more. Jesus was powerful, but that was never his focus. His power came from his relationship with his Heavenly Father—the only authentic source. Where and how do you feel powerful? Are the consequences of your power destructive or constructive?

Portland

People often talk about feeling a void in their lives. They try all kinds of ways to fill the void—work, food, sex, activity. But knowing and accepting God's love is the only real opportunity to fill the void. His love won't fluctuate. It's not prone to the weakness and frailty that we see in human love. What have you tried substitute for love, to fill the void? What difference does God's love make in your everyday life?

Stress, peace and focus

As human beings we set goals, make plans, project ahead and progress on our own power. When something goes wrong, we get frantic and start pulling strings to try to regain stability. When that fails, we panic. We fail to wait on the Lord. We forget that He has a plan that doesn't always parallel ours. We don't trust Him to be always moving on our behalf. In the dance with God, we forget who leads, and the resulting pressure and stress causes us needless anxiety. When asked by God to wait, how do you handle it? When did you think that God had forgotten you and left you, only to find out later that He was actually leading you into something special?

Chester's church

The richness of God's creation is always close around us, within the ordinary lives of the people we come in contact with. Everything we do in relationship to other people adds to or subtracts from that richness, sometimes in surprising ways. This is the excitement of life. If we are not sensitized to the opportunities that exist around us for the advancement of God's kingdom, we may miss them. The more regularly we depend on God for His guidance, the less likely we are to miss opportunities to bring joy and encouragement into the world. Hunter admonishes us to simply, "Obey Him," so as to become a constructive and loving part of the big picture. Have you ever failed to take advantage of an opportunity that God has provided to you? If the choices in life are either to expand or withdraw in partnership with God, what direction is your life taking?

A beautiful day in the neighborhood

Hunter's stories of his Long Beach neighborhood are often harsh, because they are rooted in the gang scene. But a neighborhood is a neighborhood, and in any neighborhood there are families, friendships, businesses, government and places of worship. Neighborhoods are part of God's plan for community, productivity, safety and the spreading of His love. So it is natural for us to celebrate community with marching bands, dancing, cool cars, good food and fellowship, even when that community is challenged by dangerous circumstances. Do you practice your faith in an isolated way, or are you part of a faith-community? What do we gain when we celebrate community? Do Jesus' friends provide a clue?

Pastor Glenn and the Love Unlimited Community Church

Our character and emotions are profoundly affected by events of the past. Those events can hurt us and keep us from having a close relationship with God. When we struggle with problems that have built up over the years, healing begins only after a very painful process of recognition and adjustment. And as Pastor Glenn points out, community is one of the gifts that God gives us to help us move down the path of true restoration. Can you identify a turning point in your life that took you in a bad direction? Did things get turned around? If so, how?

Chapter 6 – San Diego

Sunshine in San Diego

God had dealt with me in Portland in 1998. But in 2000, He really got serious with me. That's when my journey really started—when God had me move here to San Diego. I told Him, *What am I gonna do in San Diego, Lord? I mean, I've got a brother there and I love him. But we are not on the same page.*

God wanted me out of Long Beach. He knew I had no one to be around there that was walkin' with the Lord. I was runnin' around with robbers, drug dealers, muggers, prostitutes, burglars—you name it. I grew up with these people. God wanted me to come out from all that and move to San Diego. It reminded me of what God told Abraham: *Abraham! Come on! Get over to a land you know nothin' about. Get out from around your kindreds, because I want to bless you.* So I said, *Well, Lord. I'll do what You say. I don't know if this will work, but I trust You. You are all I have.* See, He *is* all I have. He is my direction. He is my leader, my guide and my protector.

At that time, I had no car—nothin'! But when I got to San Diego, God gave me favor with my younger brother Robert, and I moved in with him and his wife and kids for a while. Robert worked at a pharmaceutical company in La Jolla, on Torrey Pines Road, and he gave me a tour. I was amazed! I told him, "Man, I could never do something like this."

But I got a job interview at another company nearby, a week later. Walking in there for the interview, I thought, *What am I doing here? They're gonna laugh at me.* Inside, the guy asked me, "What's your name?" When he said that, I almost turned around and walked out. But I said, "I'm August

Hunter." He said, "We know about you. The job is yours. We'll train you." A week later I was working as an environmental safety inspector in the labs, wearing a white coat. Their Human Resources people still can't figure out how I got in there! That job lasted about eight months and it gave me a good start in San Diego. I got to know a lot of people there, and I even started Bible studies in the labs.

The Neil Good Day Center

The sinful mind is hostile to God. It does not submit to God's law, nor can it do so.

Romans 8

[The Neil Good Day Center is a facility for the homeless located in east San Diego.]

So I started my job in San Diego, I was attending the Rock Church, I was doing Bible studies—everything was goin' good. Then one day me and my brother were riding along in his truck. We were downtown on 17th Street, by the Neil Good Day Center. I said, "Man Robert, look at all these homeless people. We ought to feed 'em!" He said, "Yeah?" I said, "Yeah. Let's go get those sandwiches," because there was this lady that lived across the street from Robert who had just died and her family was having a funeral session at their house and they had all these sandwiches that they didn't use and they brought them across the street to give to us, and these sandwiches were sitting on our kitchen counter.

So we drove back home and got those forty or fifty sandwiches and brought them back to the Center. As soon as we jumped out of Robert's truck and those homeless people saw the sandwiches, they formed a line. Robert started handing out the sandwiches and I just started praying with the people and saying, "God bless you," you know? They would say, "Aw, this is cool!" Then after the sandwiches ran out, we looked at the line and there was a hundred more people. I asked Robert, "What should we do?" He said,

"Let's go to Albertson's and get two hundred pieces of that cooked chicken and some loaves of bread and come back." I said, "Wow! Let's do that!" So like clockwork we got the chicken and bread and got back to the Center. The people were still there and when we drove up they came running and formed a line again and I continued ministering to them and we handed out the chicken and bread. We had enough chicken and bread for the amount of people that were there, so after they all got their food, we sat there and fellowshipped with them. It was awesome!

When I first came to San Diego I met my friend Roger Zeigler in a Bible study. One day I was at Roger's house and I told him, "Me and my brother went down to this place called the Neil Good Day Center where homeless people can wash their clothes, make phone calls, cut their hair, and watch TV—and we fed them." Roger said, "I always wanted to feed the homeless." I said, "Let's tell more people, and then let's do it!" So Roger announced it at the Bible study, "We are feeding the homeless this weekend."

We used Roger's kitchen to birth that homeless ministry. Our whole group would meet at Roger's house on Saturday morning and cook all the food, in his kitchen. We always had fruit and salad and bread and the main course. We might make spaghetti and garlic bread.

This became routine and the people at the Center knew we were coming on Saturday. I would prepare a little sermon. Roger would have these tables and chairs set up where the people could eat. The ladies and the guys who were part of our ministry would be there, ready to serve the food. I would deliver my sermon on this raised part of the outside courtyard, then pray over the food and then we would eat. We'd bring Bible tracts and hand out Bible tracts and just minister to the people and hang out with them the whole day. I mean, we were doing a big work down there! I was so fired up because I was doing what God had called me to do—start a Bible study and start a homeless ministry.

As time went on, things were just goin' at a flow. But one Saturday we go down to the Neil Good Day Center with our group. We feed the homeless people like always. When everything is over, our group steps out through the gate of the courtyard and we all stand on the sidewalk for a while, just fellowshipping. But then I look across the street and I see my brother sitting in his truck with his family. They were getting ready to pull out and leave, but now my brother is blasting his truck horn—*BAW! BAW! BAW!*—and he is pointing through the windshield of his truck at something up the street, and I can see his mouth yelling, "August! August! August!"

I look up the street and I see a young lady from our group—a tall girl with dark hair—and she has strayed off and tried to minister to a guy who was just walking along that street. I can see that the guy is all buffed out—his muscles are showing out from under his tank top—and he looks like he just got out of jail. He has grabbed this tall lady by one arm and is running his hand through her pants pockets for money. So my brother is blowin' his horn and I see the situation. I look at our people—Roger and everybody— and the Lord tells me, *You know they ain't gonna run over there. Get over there!*

So I head across the street, toward the guy. When this guy sees me coming, he grabs this lady by her pants pocket and jerks her behind his back and holds her there. I can see from his eyes that he has gone five or six nights without sleeping.

I say to him, "Hey, man! What's goin' on?"

"Hey, MF! Get outta my face, you MF!"

I think, *Oh, Lord*. See, you have to understand that when this happened, I am still a fresh baby Christian and it won't take much for me to reach out and touch this guy with a live wire. I am watching this guy's hands when he talks and moves, and if it looks like he's gonna clock me, I'm gonna clock him first.

Then a scripture comes to my mind, how the Devil tries to encourage you to do his work. In the eighth chapter of Romans, it says that your mind is an enemy to God. So I am standing there and the Devil says, *Well, go ahead and chin-check him one time and pick him up and throw him over that fence there and you won't have nothin' to worry about.* I look back at our group and they are looking at me like, *What are you going to do, August?* And I look at the homeless people that we just fed standing in the courtyard, looking out through the bars of the fence and their faces are like, *Okay Preacher. You fed us. Now you gonna beat that guy down?* And the dude just keeps huffin' and puffin' and cussin' at me.

I think, *Wow, Lord.*

The Lord says to me, *Tell him that I love him.*

I think, *Lord, this man does not want to hear that. He wants to fight, man.*

Tell- him- that- I- love- him. That is power.

I stand there a little while and then I say, "You know, man, the Lord loves you."

He says, "What?! You MF! You MF!" then, "Oh, man—phew,…"

I wait a little and then I tell him again, "God loves you, man."

He goes, "Eh! Ah! Ah!,…" and then starts cryin' and breakin' down. He lets go of the lady and then tries to hug me. I think, *Get back, dude,* but he grabs me and says, "Nobody never told me that!" and he falls to his knees, sobbin'. Everybody in our group comes over and he stands up cryin' and says, "God loves me!" I think, *Wow! That's all it took?*

That was the beginning of our *Bread of Life* ministry at the Rock Church, and it's one of the biggest ministries that they have today, the feed-the-homeless ministry. I tell you, we nourished that ministry. See, one thing I learned about God is that when you are looking for God to bless something, you've got to already have something for Him to bless. If you're looking for God to bless something, you've got to already be doing something. God is not going to take nothing and then bless it. It's got to be something that He can multiply. In Mark, Jesus went to his hometown and the people there rejected him, so he could not perform any miracles there. Why was that? It was because those people were not already recognizing and doing the things of God. To them Jesus was just a carpenter, Mary's son. They were not interested in God's business. So there was nothing for Him to bless. Nothing. Just unbelief.

When you appreciate the things of God—you believe God, you trust God, you have confidence in God—God can take and multiply that. God can make miracles happen out of that. But you've got to have something for God to bless. You've got to be doing something. He doesn't just *make* something happen. *You* have got to be about His business. And when you're about God's business, God is going to be about your business.

Moving out and up

> *Then Joseph said to his brothers, "Come close to me." When they had done so, he said, "I am your brother Joseph, the one you sold into Egypt! And now, do not be distressed and do not be angry with yourselves for selling me here, because it was to save lives that God sent me ahead of you."*

> *Genesis 45*

As time went on in San Diego, I became part of more ministries. I met Ron Moreno, who had me working with high school kids at Magnolia Wesleyan Church, about the time they had the shooting at the high school in that area. And Pastor John Leeder—he was incarcerated at one time—was asking me to do prison ministry. Roger and I were still doing our stuff together, and I was worshiping at the Rock Church. I was trying to stay on the straight and narrow path.

But I was going through some stuff with my family. I had lived at my brother's house for almost a year. Things were going bad there and I had a falling out with them. It was time for me to move on. My dad was part of that mess. He involved himself in it. He judged me on the things I was doing and that devastated me, him being a man of God. I thought it was something that they all were doing together because they didn't like me or they wanted to hurt me.

After I moved out of my brother's house, I stayed with a guy who was in our Bible study, but he was in the military and was getting ready to ship out, so I had just a month to stay at his place. Then some friends of mine who were in the music business called me out of nowhere and sent me a ticket to come to Oklahoma. I had never been to Oklahoma. I stayed out in Oklahoma about three weeks and I enjoyed myself. They sent me back to San Diego with fifteen-hundred dollars so I was able to get myself a room. I was homeless—living in that room—for a good while, but I was happy. I had a roof over my head. Roger would come and pick me up for his Bible study, Ron would come pick me up for Magnolia Wesleyan Church and John would come and pick me up for the prison ministry.

I began to understand what was going on. God was taking me to a whole new level. I know today that when God is ready to take you to a new level, he lets things happen—to move you, to get you where He wants you. Like when He made me leave Long Beach to get to San Diego, God was shuttin' everything down for me—my place in Long Beach wouldn't rent to me anymore, there was killin' goin' on, just crazy stuff—so I had to leave. God was allowing this stuff with my brother, to move me where He wanted me to be so He can bless me.

At first I was angry with my brother and my dad for putting me in that situation. But as I grew in Christ, God helped me understand that it wasn't their doing. It was God's doing.

I relate this to the story of Joseph and his brothers. God embedded character in Joseph, and that meant that Joseph could forgive people and see God at work in his circumstances. Joseph's dad, Jacob, made him a coat of many colors and Joseph's brothers hated him for that. They beat Joseph and threw him in a pit. One of them had the idea, "We can sell him to the Midianites—get some money off of him," and the Midianites took Joseph down to Egypt.

Potiphar, who was a captain in the Egyptian army, bought Joseph and took him to his house. Potiphar was a man who could see God in the midst of his business, and he saw that everything Joseph touched was blessed. But the reason that everything Joseph touched was blessed was that Joseph had forgiven his brothers for beatin' him up and throwin' him in the pit and sellin' him.

Then Potiphar's wife came on to Joseph and wanted him to lay with her. And this is where Joseph's integrity came in. He said, "Should I do this and sin against God?" His integrity stood up. Joseph fled and they caught Joseph, because Potiphar's wife said that Joseph tried to rape her, and they threw Joseph in jail.

Joseph went to jail and the jailer connected with Joseph. And everybody that was in the jail was blessed because of Joseph. The reason is—Joseph had forgiven Potiphar's wife for what she had done to get him incarcerated in the first place. He had forgiven her. And so by him forgiving her, he opened the door for God to come in and bless him, so that Joseph could bless everybody in prison. So the jailer loved Joseph. Everybody in jail loved Joseph, because they were blessed.

Then Joseph found himself incarcerated with Pharaoh's baker and butler after Pharaoh had them arrested, and Joseph interpreted their dreams. Joseph told the baker that his dream meant that Pharaoh was going to chop his head off, but told the butler that God was going to restore him back to being Pharaoh's cupbearer, or whatever he was. And it all happened. But Joseph had told the butler, "When you get back up to Pharaoh, don't forget about me." But the butler *did* forget about him, and Joseph ended up staying down there two more years, until Pharaoh had a dream that needed to be interpreted and the butler said, "Oh yeah! There's this Hebrew down in the jail that interpreted my dream. He's a dream interpreter. Call him, Pharaoh! He can help you." Pharaoh had Joseph cleaned up and brought to him and he got up there and Pharaoh told him the dream and Joseph interpreted the dream and Pharaoh took Joseph and made him prime minister over all Egypt.

Why do I share that story? It is because when God wants to do something with you, he'll shut one door and open up another, so he can get you to where He wants you, where He can bless you. Joseph did not know that he would have to go through all those things before God could get him where He needed him. But God was with Joseph everywhere he went. So I don't hold that stuff against my brother or my dad. I don't hold that against them, because I know that God lets things happen so that you can be a blessing to those that come after you.

Forgiveness

If you love, you must forgive. I have learned: You can't love someone without forgiving them. And you can't forgive someone without loving them.

Loveandforgiveness

If you forgive a person, that will help you love them, despite what they do to you. Love and forgiveness should have been one word: *loveandforgiveness*.

Unforgiveness

Unforgiveness is like a cancer that eats you from the inside. It will make you sick. You have to take control of unforgiveness. Get that junk out of you! You might be walkin' around dyin' because of what some other individual did to you years back. God might even allow you to observe that individual who hurt you being blessed and moving ahead. That individual might just prosper and prosper and prosper—and yet you are stagnating because you will not forgive, you will not do it God's way.

Jonah's unforgiveness

> *When God saw what [the Ninevites] did and how they turned from their evil ways, he had compassion and did not bring upon them the destruction he had threatened. But Jonah was greatly displeased and became angry. He prayed to the LORD, "O LORD, is this not what I said when I was still at home? That is why I was so quick to flee to Tarshish. I knew that you are a gracious and compassionate God, slow to anger and abounding in love, a God who relents from sending calamity. Now, O LORD, take away my life, for it is better for me to die than to live."*

> *Jonah 3, 4*

[Brian, mentioned by Hunter below, was a young California prison inmate who swallowed a packet of crystal meth while being searched by a prison guard. Brian hallucinated wildly for three days on the floor of a prison holding tank, soaked in his own sweat.]

I was reading about Jonah's unforgiveness. God's wrath was ready to come down on the Ninevites because of the way they were operating. God gave instructions to Jonah to go down to Nineveh and preach to the Ninevites, so that the Ninevites would change their ways and be saved. But Jonah had hate and unforgiveness for the Ninevites because the Ninevites had killed some of his people, and Jonah did not want God to save the Ninevites.

So instead of obeying God by going to Nineveh, Jonah caught a boat for Tarshish. But because of Jonah's disobedience, God brought a storm down on that boat, and everybody on that boat was scared. They yelled, "Everybody! Call on your god!" They cast lots to find the troublemaker, and Jonah got found out. They asked Jonah, "Man, what did you do?" Jonah told them, "I'm running from God." Now, I scratched my head when I read that. I thought, *How can you run from God? He is everywhere.* But then God showed me that Jonah really was running when Jonah became disobedient. Disobedience separates you from God. When disobedience separates you from God, you are no longer walking with God. You are out there on your own.

So the other men threw Jonah off that boat into the water. And God had a big fish to swallow Jonah. And in the belly of that fish, Jonah started praying, something he should have been doing from the beginning. He prayed for three days. And God had the big fish spit Jonah up on dry land and Jonah came to his senses and got down to Nineveh and preached the word of God to the Ninevites. So Jonah went through some stuff—he got thrown off a boat, he got swallowed up by a big fish and he finally did what God said to do. So God was able to forgive the Ninevites and they were saved.

But Jonah got angry when God saved the Ninevites. He told God, "Let me die! I know the God that you are. That's why I didn't want to go down to Nineveh and preach, because I knew you would save those guys." That tripped me out. I could see that Jonah never turned loose that unforgiveness. He was still carrying that stuff around. He even had enough nerve to tell God he wanted to die. That's the nature of unforgiveness. It's ugly! It's nasty! Jonah had that stuff in him so bad that God let Jonah just wallow in his anger. He let Jonah soak in his anger like Brian was soaking in his own sweat. God allowed Jonah to deal with his own feelings, and Jonah was able to see himself.

When you don't do things God's way, it makes your way rough. Nothing is going to work for you. You put pressure on yourself. You are doing it like Jonah—you are running from God. God will bring you to a place where you can see yourself and you can repent, and things will come out so much better. God tells us, *If you don't forgive, I can't forgive you. Straight up!* But as long as you hold on to that unforgiveness, you will be just like Jonah.

Caught up in your unforgiveness

> *Jesus said, "Father, forgive them, for they do not know what they are doing." And they divided up his clothes by casting lots.*

Luke 23

> *While they were stoning him, Stephen prayed, "Lord Jesus, receive my spirit." Then he fell on his knees and cried out, "Lord, do not hold this sin against them." When he had said this, he fell asleep.*

Acts 7

You should not leave up out of this world wrapped up in your unforgiveness. You have got to get that stuff out of you. Get that anger, that animosity, that unforgiveness out of you. Jesus was on the cross and they were right there in front of him, killing him. But Jesus wasn't going to leave up out of here with something in his heart towards them. He cried out, "Father, forgive them, for they do not know what they are doing." And Paul had Stephen stoned to death. But Stephen looked up and saw Jesus on the right hand of God, and Stephen said, "Lord, do not hold this sin against them." Stephen was leavin' up out of this world. He was gettin' ready to be with the Father. He did not want to leave with anything on his heart. So you don't want to leave up out of here with unforgiveness on your heart.

Room for God

When we love an individual who hurts us, that gives God room to come into a situation—to do whatever He has to do to bring that hurtful individual in, to break that individual down. God says He will never forsake us. He will fight our battles. So we have to give the situation to Him and let Him come in and do what He wants. Until we come to that point, the situation will remain the same. It will even get worse. See, when we try to hold on to stuff against that individual, we are trying to defend ourselves. We are telling God, *Naw, I got it.* And then God can't come in. He can't come in when we don't give Him the situation.

I tell you, the job of loving gets hard. But if we don't forgive, it *really* gets hard. You know? You love people and then they can continue to operate out of their nasty way, that nasty disposition, still trying to hurt you in the midst of you loving them. And you think, *Wow, man. They just don't get it.* And it hurts. It hurts and it definitely gets hard. I struggled with that for a long time. I still struggle as I try to love my dad. Even though I suffer in the midst of what he does, I love him, because God calls me to love. He calls each of us to love that way. If we are going to please God, we have *got* to love. I really struggled, until I learned that love has another word that goes with it—forgiveness. That made it easier for me to love.

The Devil will have you thinking

It is hard for you to love an individual who has been hurting you time and time and time again. You want to forgive, but this individual was just nasty with you in the past. He did spiteful things to you all your life. That is a hard job.

The strangest thing is, the Devil tries to keep you stuck in that. The Devil will have you looking at that stuff and considering it. He'll tell you, "Man, you're gonna forgive *him*? Naw, you can't just let *that* go. He hurt you! He cheated you! He robbed you! You're gonna let that go? You need to get even!" The Devil will have you thinking like that.

Heart and mind

That's why your mind must be transformed. You must put on the mind of Christ. When you put on the mind of Christ, you can keep your heart clean. Otherwise we let that unforgiveness get filtered through our mind and it gets in our heart and it becomes a stronghold there, and then we have Hell on our hands. Guard your heart. When you put on the mind of Christ, you operate out of a clean heart. And out of the abundance of the heart, the mouth speaks.

When you put on the mind of Christ, you are not looking at things from your perspective. *Your* perspective! That's the Devil playin' with you, playin' with your mind, having you look at things in a vengeful way. But when you put on the mind of Christ, you are looking at things from God's perspective. You're looking at things from the eyes of God. You are looking past the individual who hurts you and seeing the need in the individual.

God shows out

So I had to make a decision. I thought, *Well, what will I be to God?* I can't be nothin' to God unless I love my enemies as myself. Was I going to hold on to all the stuff that was done to me, or let it go and walk with Jesus? Will I go down the path of me holding on to unforgiveness and getting even with people, or will I take the Jesus-path? So I decided I'm going to love people. And you know what? By me forgiving them, that gives me a genuine love for them.

Now I'm excited, because I do not try to fight a situation myself. I give it to God. I trust Him and I let Him handle it. And God shows up and shows out. God shows up when I forgive and give Him room to come in. Amen? And by Him dealing with the situation, He shows out. He shows up and He shows out. That's what He does, because He's God!

This is serious

> *Rescue those being led away to death; hold back those staggering toward slaughter.*
>
> *Proverbs 24*

I have quite a few little nephews growing up now that are trying to glamorize the life I had when I was a gangster back in their neighborhood. They admire the gangbanging lifestyle they see back there. If you are a young guy like they are, you develop a taste for that gangbanging stuff in the neighborhood, especially if some of the *hard* gangsters respect you because at one time your uncle came through there and put in some work. If you have an uncle that the hard gangsters look up to, that's like an American Express card for a young guy that is seeking that lifestyle. When gangsters in the neighborhood are saying, "You know whose nephew that is?" you get that extra good treatment.

I do not want my nephews thinking, *My uncle was a shotcaller for the Rollin' 20's Crips, so nobody will mess with me.* I don't want them lost and consumed by that. That could become a way of life for them and that would not be cool, because that leaves them in a position where they will be challenged. So I decided that while I was here in San Diego, I had to get them out of that frame of mind, because they were still living there in Long Beach and they were depending on my name.

I started shuttin' all that down. I told my nephews, "You don't allow *nobody* to refer to me as Big Dog. You tell them my name is August." That turned them off. They said, "Oh no. That's your name. You're Big Dog." I said, "No, no, no." I had to deal with that, because that was something that I created. I was responsible for that.

One of my sisters has three boys. I love these boys and I didn't know what their outcome would be. The oldest one just got his life together. The littlest one got a chance to play ball, and he is a football star in Illinois. But the middle one was headed into gangbangin'—big time. He is a leader, like I was. The guys his age respect him because he is a fighter. He was coming up the same way I did. I saw myself in him.

Pretty soon the rival gang was coming to my nephew's school and shooting at him. They were trying to kill him. He called me to say, "They are coming here—shootin' at me!" I knew it was serious, and I told my sister,

"The kid's life is in danger." She didn't understand, so I knew I had to grab this kid. I pulled him out of Long Beach—about three years ago when I was living on 65th Street—because his life was so similar to mine when I was coming up. I just snatched him up out of Long Beach and brought him here to San Diego.

His mother was so hot at me for that. But then the guy my nephew was runnin' with—the rival gang caught up with him at school and killed him. They would have killed my nephew too if he had been there, but I had him here in San Diego. My sister called me crying and said, "This is serious!" I said, "I've been tryin' to tell you that!"

So I had my middle nephew staying with me, going to school. I helped him. I was able to get him on the right track.

The murder of Tracy Brown

My friend Tracy Brown got out of federal prison in 2002. He found out that I was living in San Diego and that I was walkin' with the Lord. He liked that, so he arranged for the homeboys to get back together with me in the old Long Beach neighborhood. We did that, and they were all going to buy me a new car the next day. But then Tracy got killed.

I first met Tracy Brown back when I got out of the penitentiary in 1986. I heard that Tracy was already in my neighborhood selling drugs, big time. I personally knew a guy that was selling drugs for Tracy, and I found out that *that* guy had beat down one of the youngsters that was selling drugs for me. I was planning to get this guy and he knew I was after him. I would drive around looking for him in this area called Poly Apartments. But whenever I would see him, he would spot my car and take off running and go hide in one of the apartments. Before I could get out of my car, he would disappear.

So one day I park my car away from the Poly Apartments and I walk in there with my Louisville Slugger. Then I see the guy and he sees me and he takes off runnin' and I take off runnin' after him. He's hollerin' and I'm gainin'. He runs up these stairs into an apartment and slams the door but I'm right behind him. *BOOM!*—I kick in the door, and there sits Tracy at the kitchen table, bagging up a whole pile of drugs.

Tracy looks at me. Then he says, "Who are you?"

I yell, "Get down on the floor!"

"Wait. Who—"

"Get on the floor before I split your wig!" and I look around. "Where he went?"

"He ran in the bedroom."

"Get him out of there!"

"Wait. I wanna—"

"I'll bust your head open!"

"Wait. I wanna give you some money."

Now Tracy has got my attention. I say, "You wanna give me money?"

"Yeah," Tracy says. "What did he do?"

"He beat down my worker."

"I'll give you three times what he took."

I say, "Well, alright."

"But I need your name."

"It's Dog."

"Dog."

"Yeah. They call me Big Dog."

Then Tracy tells me, "I wanna join teams with you."

We start talkin' and we get friendly. He had heard people talk about me. People were telling him, "Big Dog's comin' home. He runs a lot of stuff around here." So Tracy knew about me, and we connected. I guess that guy stayed back there in that bedroom the whole time.

Tracy was a piece of work. He was the type of dude you could trust. If Tracy was with you, he was *with* you. He would never run out on me. That's why we had such a good friendship.

Tracy had made it really big, selling drugs for a long time. When I came home from prison in 1986, he had all this stuff—a Mercedes Benz, a big BMW, boats and jet skis. He had a slant-nose, ragtop Porsche Carrera—aw, it was really nice! And Tracy was a lady's man. He had a way with women.

One time I went with Tracy back to Baltimore, which was his old neighborhood. He got permission from his parole officer to fly back there. When we got to the baggage claim, there were police and undercover cops everywhere. They had Tracy's photograph. They jacked us up, looking through all our suitcases. They found Tracy's special Rolex watch, which was *pervaded* with diamonds. It had so many diamonds in it, it just looked crazy! The policeman said, "Man, look at this!" Tracy told him, "Yeah. If that watch was real, it'd be worth a lot." Then the policeman said, "If this was real— shoot—it would be worth a couple hundred thousand." Well, that watch *was* worth that, with all the money Tracy put into it. It *was* real. He had that kind of money. When we got out of the airport I told Tracy, "Man, don't *ever* take that watch anywhere with us! It's trouble."

We stayed with Tracy's family a few weeks. I beat down some guy at a club because he disrespected us. I was drunk and Tracy said, "August, you better beat him down." I said, "I *am* gonna beat him down." That's all I remember. When I woke up back at Tracy's house, I had blood all over my pants and shirt. I asked Tracy, "What happened?" He said, "You beat that guy down and we put you in the car and you went right to sleep. Then we put you in bed and here you are now." Some cops that went to high school with Tracy had broken up the fight. They told him, "Tracy, take him home."

After we got back to California, that's when I violated my parole by throwing that girl through the window at the club, and I went back to prison.

123

In 1989 the feds came to get Tracy. He got locked up from 1989 to 2002. He lost all his stuff. His girlfriend ran off with the Rolex.

When Tracy got out of prison in 2002, he wanted to get back into that whole drug scene. I didn't know that, because by that time I was doing ministry here in San Diego. He was out of prison seven or eight months, doing that stuff again. And then he got killed.

It happened one day when this guy I knew—his name was Trouble—came down to San Diego to pick me up and drive me back to Long Beach, to the Westside. Tracy liked what I was doing with my life and he told me that he would send Trouble to come get me and we would all get together and they would buy me a new car the next day. When I got to Long Beach, it was me and One Round and Trouble, at Trouble's mom's house. Me and One Round waited for Tracy in her front yard. One Round started drinking Jack Daniels straight from the bottle and then Tracy got there, so we were talking to Tracy; Trouble was inside his mom's house. Tracy got into an argument on his cell phone with this girl I knew. He handed me the phone and said, "August, talk to her." I told her, "I know he'll pay you back." She kept saying, "That was my money I was saving." I finally got off the phone and it was getting dark outside.

Then—and I remember this like it was yesterday—I look down the block. I see movement. I see a guy. He is wearing a black hooded sweatshirt, black pants and black sneakers. I know this type of suit. We call it a "do low suit" for when you do low-down things at night. I see that this guy is walkin' slow with his hands in his pockets and that hood over his head. My spirit starts speakin' to me, you know? I keep lookin', and Tracy and One Round keep talkin'. But then they see that I'm not payin' attention to them and Tracy turns around to see what I'm lookin' at and he sees the guy, but he turns back like he ain't seen nothin'. Then things go into slow motion—like I am in a trance—and the guy is walkin' real slow and my spirit speaks, *When*

August Hunter - *LORD OF LONG BEACH*

that guy gets here, he's gonna start shootin'. I think, *Man, these guys are so comfortable,* because I never get comfortable where things can happen so fast.

The guy is right by us now and he pulls up his sweatshirt and takes hold of a big gun that is tucked into his belt and he points that gun right at Tracy's face and I see it's a .45 automatic with an extended clip. I yell, "Look out!" and I turn to run. Then *BOOM!* and I see foot-long yellow fire come out the barrel of that gun and I see Tracy grab his cheek with two hands. Tracy turns to run, then *BOOM-BOOM-BOOM!* he gets shot in his back. Tracy falls to the ground, and somehow I fall on my stomach next to him. I open my eyes and see the guy standing right over Tracy. Then he fires more shots into Tracy's back. That gun is right there by me and I think about grabbin' it, but I can see that the guy's eyes are like red devil-eyes. I am layin' there, but he doesn't shoot me. Then it's quiet. The guy looks at Tracy for a while. Then he turns and runs off with the gun. I don't know where One Round is.

Trouble runs out of the house and says, "Aw man!" and takes off his jacket and puts it over Tracy and Tracy is saying, "August—Ah—August!" I am laying there next to him and I say, "Tracy. Don't talk, man." That's all I can say to him because now all the people on the block are running out of their houses with their automatics, loading a round—*AKK-AKK! AKK-AKK!* I am worried because I have not been around this stuff for a few years and I don't know who's who. People ask, "Where he went, Big Dog?" and some people run down the alley after the guy. One Round is standing there now and Tracy says, "One Round—You set me up?" One Round says, "No, man! I didn't set you up." That's when the gang police come and there's nothing else we can do, because they are sweatin' us. After the ambulance leaves, I wait at Trouble's mom's house for about three hours.

All during that shooting, the Lord was speaking to me: *Look at what can happen in this world. You see what Tracy has got to deal with. He rejected me. You are covered by my blood. But I can't protect you if you don't stay close.* It was like that guy in the sweatshirt never saw me laying there. He never looked at me—not once. And that doesn't happen in that neighborhood. When something like that occurs, they don't leave witnesses. They just don't.

That guy gunned Tracy down, but Tracy didn't die right there. He died at the hospital. My sister took me there. When I got there, Tracy's family was in a circle around him, praying. I joined them. When we finished, Tracy died. It was sad, you know, for Tracy to leave up out of here like that. It messed me up. I got myself back to San Diego. I still have the newspaper clipping from when he was killed. I looked at it just the other day.

Getting ahead of God's anointing

You love righteousness and hate wickedness; therefore God, your God, has set you above your companions by anointing you with the oil of joy.

Psalm 45

We need to wait for God before we act. We need to wait for God's anointing—His blessing—on our actions. Because it's not about our timing; it's about God's timing. God works outside of time. We work inside of time. So we have to wait for Him. Otherwise we get ahead of God's anointing.

Moses got ahead of God's anointing. God had a plan for Moses to deliver the children of Israel out of slavery in Egypt. As part of that plan, God placed Moses into Pharaoh's household. But Moses decided he wasn't going to stay in Pharaoh's house and he went down to be together with the children of Israel. Then he killed an Egyptian, which wasn't in God's plan. Moses had to flee for his life into the wilderness, because he got ahead of God's anointing.

When the right time came, God showed Himself to Moses on a mountain, in a burning bush. God let Moses see the bush burning and that the bush wasn't being consumed by the fire—God got Moses' attention at just the right time. Then God dealt with Moses and told Moses to get down to Egypt. When Moses got himself down to Egypt, God's anointing went ahead of Moses—to protect Moses, to open up the door for him with Pharaoh. Because of that, Moses was able to stand before Pharaoh, he was able to confront Pharaoh, he was able to tell Pharaoh what God had said. And Moses could *keep* coming before Pharaoh and *keep* bringing curses and plagues. Moses didn't have to flee from Pharaoh, because he didn't get ahead of God's anointing; God's anointing was ahead of him.

When you get out ahead of God's anointing, you are out there by yourself. You are not under God's protection. You are not under God's power. We need to learn how to wait-up on God. And when we wait-up on God, it's God's anointing that will go before us and open up the door.

Nehemiah was a man who waited for God's anointed time. Nehemiah was in exile under King Artaxerxes, and he heard that back home the walls of Jerusalem were burnt down. Nehemiah was worried by that. His heart was involved. He wanted to do something about that.

Now Nehemiah had a personal relationship with King Artaxerxes—he was the king's cupbearer—and he could have gone straight to the king when he got the news, to get help. But no. Nehemiah waited, and he cried out to God, and he started praying and fasting. Finally God spoke to Nehemiah and told him to go to the king. And when the king finally saw him, Nehemiah didn't even need to open up his mouth, because God's grace was all over him. King Artaxerxes only had to look at Nehemiah.

The king said, "Nehemiah, your countenance don't look right. And I know you're not sick."

Nehemiah said, "No. I'm not sick."

The king said, "Well, there's *somethin'* wrong."

Nehemiah said, "The walls of Jerusalem burnt down, King. I desire to go there."

The king said, "Well, how long will it take you? What do you need? How many people do you need to help you?" God not only gave Nehemiah favor with the king, but He had the king supply Nehemiah with all his needs. That was because Nehemiah waited on God.

I compare all this to me being here in San Diego. I first came here to San Diego in the 1980s, to sell drugs. You see what I'm saying? I got ahead of God's anointing. And because I didn't have God's anointing, I had to flee, like Moses did when he killed that Egyptian. I had to hide out from the other gangs and the police.

Then God had me go back to New Orleans and to Portland, to learn about Him. And once I learned about Him, God sent me back to San Diego in 2000, this time with His anointing going before me. God prepared a place for me at my brother's house and I started making ministries and God opened up the prison doors for me and He got me to be a member at the Rock Church and before you know it I came onto the Rock Church staff. All that was because I didn't get ahead of the anointing. I allowed the anointing to go before me.

We need to realize that God has got something for each of us that will blow our mind. He wants you to say, "Wow Lord!" So when I have trouble, I don't worry, I don't get confused, I don't get disappointed. I know what God is doing. Any time he closes one door, he opens up another. In the meantime, I can cool my heels and enjoy life. I know he's got something for me. And whatever He has for me, I'll be compatible with it, involved in it, connected to it.

Chapter 6 Study Guide

Sunshine in San Diego

We live in a time where many of us no longer expect miracles. We have so much at our disposal that we quit looking to God for the unexpected. But the miraculous does happen. God opens doors, puts just the right person in our path or whispers an answer to us. We need to be open to God's miracles and give Him thanks when we are surprised by them. When has something happened to you that was clearly a miraculous gift from God? What gets in your way of recognizing God's touch in your life? Are you too busy to notice, too rational to believe, too controlling to not take credit?

The Neil Good Day Center

What do you want me to do here, Lord? That is a question we forget to ask. Each day we have the freedom to take actions and make decisions, in any way we want. Some of us have gotten into bad habits in conducting our daily lives. Our behavior can be automatic or misguided in so many ways. In living that way, we miss opportunities to hear God's voice and to do His work. Even in the most pressure-packed situations, we need to ask this question. Do you consult with God throughout the day, as if you were checking with a trusted friend? What is keeping you from checking with God about the daily decisions in your life?

Moving out and up

God communicates through circumstances. In doing so, He often cuts us off from what we are currently attached to. To us, that may seem unfair or even frightening, and human nature keeps us from letting go easily. But if we trust God, we know that He is always moving us forward. We know that we are in the flow of God's plan for us. If we go with the flow, we will move toward that which God has prepared for us downstream. In looking back over your life, when have you resisted something coming to an end, only to realize retrospectively, that the end was needed for a new beginning? Do you remember God's presence in your life during times of change and confusion?

Forgiveness

Healing—emotional healing and physical healing—was at the heart of Jesus' ministry. Today, that healing is, or at least should be, at the center of the Christian faith. Hunter's formula for healing, drawn from both his experiences and Biblical teaching, is to link our love for others to our forgiveness of them. We cannot love others, and thereby become healed ourselves, unless we recognize the imperfect state of our fellow human beings, as well as our own. Once we see them through God's eyes, we can begin to love and forgive. Are you stuck in a state of unforgiveness in relation to an important person in your life? Accordingly, are you kept from loving them?

This is serious

August started out as "Big Dog." In the same way, in the New Testament, Paul started out as "Saul of Tarsus," a sort of gangster who had the power to have people killed. But God saw Saul's heart and knew that He could use Saul's intelligence and drive to save others, just as God used those traits in August to save his nephew.

To get Saul's attention, God made Saul hit bottom, on the road to Damascus. God may likewise bring us to a low point, to help us realize that we are on the wrong track. It may take pain to alert us—a divorce, a DUI conviction, a lost job. But God will provide a way out, if we are humbled enough to realize the danger we face. How have you been lost in life? How did God call you back? Is there some dangerous part of your lifestyle that you are clinging to?

The murder of Tracy Brown

Some things happen in life that just can't be explained by ordinary conditions. People show up to help us when no one should be there, we take the wrong exit on the freeway and avoid a major wreck, someone utters just the right words when they know nothing of our situation. Nonbelievers would call this luck or coincidence. As believers, we come to know the earmarks of God's protection and intervention. We can never explain it. But we recognize it and give thanks for it as a sign of God's personal love for us.

Such protection can come under dramatic conditions, as it did for Hunter in this story. When it does come, it can be God's lesson to us regarding the important choices we are making in life. Hunter's experience revealed to him the important difference between the path he had chosen and the one chosen by his friend Tracy. Have you had experiences where it was obvious that God protected you? Are you making choices in your life that make it difficult for God to protect you?

Getting ahead of God's anointing

The things of daily life simply begin and end—TV shows, microwave meals, dating relationships, jobs, school, and so on. But God's work with us continues forever. The pattern of our daily lives, and the mindset it creates, can drive us to destruction if we don't account for God's long term plan in our lives. We may not even consider submitting our own short term plans for His review. Rather, we go full speed ahead and wonder why we end up in trouble. God might even have wanted for us what *we* wanted; but by rushing ahead, we miss His blessing. What project have you undertaken that you took on by yourself? What was the process like, and what has been the outcome?

Chapter 7 – Back in Prison

Breaking into prison

[R.J. Donovan State Prison is a high security prison near San Diego that houses approximately five thousand male inmates.]

I started doing prison ministry in San Diego around 2000 or 2001, because I met Pastor John Leeder. John had been incarcerated at one time; I could show you pictures of him in prison and you would not know it was him. But by the time I met him, Pastor John was going into Donovan Prison, ministering to the inmates there.

John told me, "August, I need you in prison ministry!"

I said, "Uh—yeah, yeah. That's good stuff there."

"Yeah, man! I'm the only one going in there. I want you in there with me."

I said, "Um. Yeah. Okay," and I walked away.

When I walked away from John, I was saying to myself, *He must be out of his mind to think I'm gonna go into somebody's prison. I'm trying to stay out of that place, not go back in!* And I kept telling myself, *Man, I am not going there! I am not goin' to no prison!* But that's not what God said. God told me I was goin'! So I went to the orientation meeting for the volunteers at Donovan Prison and I got my security clearance to go into the prison with John.

Doing prison ministry made me look back on all the stuff that I saw and did all my life. My old neighborhood messed up a lot of people. A lot of good people in that neighborhood got killed over unnecessary stuff, stuff that wasn't even worth anything.

And I lost a lot of friends who did the killing. Most everybody I knew were killers. It was just normal. I watch the TV news and I see people killin' people and I think about the reality of that, and I think, *I grew up with dudes like that.* All I can do now is thank God that I never did anything like that. There were many times when I got into an altercation and someone would put a gun in my hand and say, "Go ahead and kill him," but I would say, "Naw. I'm not gonna do that." The youngsters would say, "Big Dog, you're gettin' soft." I'd say, "No. I'm not gettin' soft." Those youngsters, they don't have a conscience. They don't have feelings. They'll kill you and go get a hamburger. It's no problem for them. The police just keep scooping them up and charging them with murders.

It wasn't until I came to Christ that I knew how foul, how crazy, how low-down that stuff was. But even before then, I would wonder why certain things happened to me. Whenever I got locked up in prison for something, I'd ask myself, *Why am I here? I did something, sure. But I am not the type of person that would do that. I get along with everybody. I don't have a race problem. I don't have a beating-a-woman problem. I've never killed no one.* I would look at the other guys in prison, and they had those issues. But I would ask, *Why am I here?*

Then God showed me that He allowed me to be incarcerated to prepare me for my work in the prison today. God allowed me to be put in the penitentiary back then. He was preparing me back then to go into prison now, to do His work. Whatever the Devil has planned for you, God always turns it into good. By me being incarcerated, God made something good develop from that, you know? It wasn't just a waste of time. God was preparing me.

Prison ministry means so much to me now. I have been incarcerated myself, so I know what the inmates in prison are going through. I know how they feel. I have walked a prison yard. I can relate to the inmates. I can love them. God instilled that love in me way back then, when He first had me go to the penitentiary.

Charley got out

Jesus said to him, "Let the dead bury their own dead, but you go and proclaim the kingdom of God."

Luke 9

[By 2005, the Rock Church had hired Hunter to do full-time prison ministry at Donovan State Prison near San Diego. Each of Donovan Prison's three main yards has its own cinderblock chapel, about forty feet square in size.]

We had this one inmate at Donovan Prison named Charley. He was the top Crip in the yard. He got his third strike for a thirty-dollar rock of cocaine. They struck him out, so he was never going home again.

Charley got cancer in prison. He went from being a great big guy down to nothin' but skin and bones. The prison would not give him a compassion release, to get out and die with his family. There was a big fuss about that among the inmates.

When Charley got cancer, he started coming into the chapel. Then one day, me and him said the sinner's prayer together, he accepted Christ, and I asked the other inmates in the chapel to baptize Charley. After that, Charley's cancer got worse—for months and months and months. He was on his way to dyin'.

Charley was searching for something. I realized what Charley was searching for in the book of Hebrews, where it talks about Abraham: "By faith he made his home in the promised land like a stranger in a foreign country." When Charley came into that prison chapel, he was a stranger there. To him, it was a foreign country. But he made an effort to live there. And Hebrews says about Abraham, "For he was looking forward to the city with foundations, whose architect and builder is God." That's what Charley was searching for—a city whose builder is God.

Then Charley died. We had Charley's memorial service in the prison chapel. The chapel was packed with inmates. They were standing along the walls, all these different gang members—Crips and Bloods, Skinheads and Mexican Mafia. These were guys that never come into the chapel, never even come to the side of the prison yard where the chapel is located.

The day of Charley's memorial service, I told myself, *Okay. Ain't none of these guys gettin' out of here before I can rap 'em across their wig.* The inmate who was leading the memorial service announced, "Come on up here in front if you want to say somethin' about Charley." I yelled, "Wait a minute! Hold up!" Then I got up in front of them and I said, "Man, I got every gangster on the yard in here and I'm gonna deal with y'all!"

I started preaching to them. I told them, "We've come here to celebrate Charley's home-goin'. But this is not a ceremony where we come to be sorrowful about Charley—he's not suffering, he's not in pain, he's not worryin' no more. My focus is on *you!* Man, y'all need to make a decision today. Each one of you has an appointment with death. There's no way around it. This body came from dirt and it's goin' back to dirt. But your spirit lives on. I pray that God will rip the heart out of your chest right now, hearin' this message. I pray that His word will convict you and the conviction will be so strong that you won't be able to sleep for weeks!" Aw man, I dealt with those guys for about an hour. I racked 'em up like pool balls and hit 'em hard! They came up and talked to me afterward. They said, "Man, I'm comin' to chapel, Pastor," and, "That was some real stuff you was talkin', man." I know that the Crips and Bloods on the yard were brought up in church—all of them. They know the truth, but they had strayed away.

So I don't like it, that the system gave Charley three strikes—a life sentence for a thirty-dollar piece of crack. But Charley touched a lot of lives before he got up out of here.

Brother C. Zachary Brewster, CIA man

Brewster—that's my boy there.

August Hunter

[California prison inmate C. Brewster provided this written contribution.]

In 2004, the Lord called August Hunter from the Rock Church in San Diego to be the pastor to the men on Yard 1 at Donovan State Prison. At that time, I—Brother C. Brewster—was the Protestant clerk in the yard chapel. When I met him, Pastor August told me that we would transform the inmates into "CIA men"—men of character, integrity and accountability.

I was raised in a Christian home. In my youth I ran track and played football. Then came a passion for lowriders and by age 17 I had my own Chevy Monte Carlo. Eventually the great Orlie himself hooked up the hydraulics on my Cadillac in Whittier, California.

But my life was undermined by the code of the street—alcohol, violence and parties. My decisions brought only drama and a fight that caused a man to be killed and then Folsom Prison. In 1988, at age 22, I got a 27-to-life prison sentence, and I would not be eligible for parole until 2004. I was overwhelmed. At Folsom, everyone around me was saying, "Don't worry. You'll get out on appeal." But I thought to myself, *I'll never survive this place. I'll get stabbed.*

In 1996 I was sitting in my cell watching Charles Stanley on TV. It was a turning point. From there I grew in Christ. I followed other inmates like Justino, Miguel and Alberto, who stepped out and took the chapel vision to the prison yard, where there was drugs, gangs and violence everywhere. We knew the mentality of the general inmate population and where the strongholds were. So in the chapel we built an alliance of Blacks, Whites and Mexicans. Folsom Prison had never seen such confidence as when 30-50 men would hold hands in a prayer circle on the prison baseball field.

One time at Folsom the housing unit officer called Chaplain Shields to tell him that something *must* be goin' down in the chapel today because a large number of young Mexican inmates were headed there. But I knew what was going on. Many times I had seen the Mexican guys walk through the yard dressed like gangsters in some prison flick, saggin' their pants but totin' their Bibles like a badge of honor. When the worship service started in the chapel, I saw Chaplain Shields praying with his eyes open. But I looked around and saw the inmates that they were worried about. I knew them all. As the worship service went on, men of all colors sang praise songs and Amazing Grace as if they wrote the songs themselves. You can always tell a man who is open to God's grace in prison—his face is soft and humble. That day there was no mean mugs or screwface; just the joy of finding something worth dying for. We inmates had worshipped money, sex and drugs, so we knew what it took to worship something. The officers looked on believing we were only there to kill each other.

When I was at Folsom, a man came into the prison to be our yard-pastor there—Reverend Moore from the Capital Christian Center in Sacramento. He taught me about the importance of service to the Body of Christ. I worked with him for my first five years and his impact in my life was rich in love and compassion. Then the news came into the prison that he would no longer be coming into the prison chapel because of aggressive skin cancer. I wept like when my step-dad died, right there in the chaplain's office. I tried to hide the tears, but they kept running down my face. Chaplain Shields said, "Take your time. Let it out." That was God working on my damaged insensitive soul. I didn't cry after my crime, or for my victim's family, because my attitude then was, *Oh well*. But now I was crying about a White man who came into my life at a time when trust was a big mountain to climb.

In 1996 Folsom had a riot between the Blacks and the Mexicans. But God covered me. It was believed that the Mexicans was gonna strike! So each day we all came out to pray out on the yard against that Spirit of Murder. When we would finish, some inmates would play baseball or exercise or lift weights in the weight pile area, and others would stay out there on the yard for a Bible study. On the day of the riot, after our prayer circle, some of the Brothers asked me to come into the weight pile area, to spot them as they lifted weights. The situation was, the prison had decided that weight lifting caused injuries to the inmates if it was not done properly, so each inmate who wanted to lift weights had to take a weight-lifting class to prevent injuries, and then he would be given a permit to enter the weight pile area, which had a fence around it with a gate. But I did not have a permit and I knew I could not get through the gate to the weight pile. But one Brother told me, "Come. She will let you in." I knew the officer they were talking about and she was strict, but I went up to the gate to prove these Brothers wrong, so that I could stay and enjoy the Bible study out on the yard. But as I walked toward the weight pile, she was nice to me and opened the gate.

Once I was inside the weight pile gate, the riot started. About two-thirds of the Mexicans out on the yard rushed toward the Black side of the yard— the basketball court and the lower area of the yard—and they also attacked the Blacks out in front of the canteen. But I was safe inside the weight pile area. There were Mexicans in there too, but they were laying on the ground, so the Blacks at the weight pile were feeling at ease about the situation. From where we were, we could hear the officers shooting with Mini-14s out from the four buildings that are in that yard and from the main guard tower. They closed down the other yards in the prison, to free up other officers to help put down the riot, and they came running. When you see a riot like that, you know it's something real bad. You can see it's not a normal fight, so you start praying.

The next time it happened I was at Donovan Prison in 2001. I was in the mess hall with other inmates, eating chow at a table. The officers that were in the mess hall ran outside into the yard. Then outside we heard, "Get down!" We all jumped up from the table and ran to the window to see what was happening. We saw Blacks beating Mexicans and Mexicans beating Blacks. The Blacks in the mess hall—mostly these young guys I knew from the chapel—they grabbed these orange plastic crates that were there; they each hold about fifty of the little milks we get at chow. But I yelled, "Put it down! Put it down! We are not doing this! Let's see what happens!" They stared at me and then put down the crates. They just stopped. It was crazy! We stayed in the mess hall, the Blacks and the Mexicans. We could hear what was happening on the other side of the mess hall door. More officers came and they pepper-sprayed the inmates outside. I guess I was a calming influence in the mess hall, but I was fed up with violence for no reason other than a misunderstanding.

After that, August came to the prison to be our yard pastor. I began to understand that God loves you no matter what, and wants to use people in spite of their past. He taught me that faith is what pleases God. It did not matter if you have a 100-year prison sentence, God was in control. We could serve Him with character, integrity and accountability, and we would grow.

Pastor August was from the hood also, so he knew what I had come through and what my potential was. He would confront me for not trusting God to release me. I had been in prison all my adult life. After 15 years in prison you are just a fixture. You have no confidence in the system or in God to change things. But then Pastor August and even the officers started asking me, "When you goin' home?"

Going home is what everyone wants, but after you have been denied that several times, you get content with your current status. But I came to understand that human identity is not a static state. It is a dynamic process, one that changes through time as an individual acquires abilities and accumulates a record of achievements and failures. I had achieved and failed, learned and lost. But I was alive and thankful, and joyful to serve others. So with Pastor August I had a real partnership. He and I worked to see men leave prison and become successful. I continued to work as his armor-bearer and administrative assistant.

In all my journey of faith, God's hand was heavy on me. Where the system said, "You ain't nobody, so die!" the Rock Church said, "You are a new creation and we love you." Where politics said, "Bury him, and forget!" the Rock Church said, "God is resurrecting you. Get ready to serve." When society said, "We ain't forgot what you did!" the Rock Church said, "We forgive you. Now do something for God." The Jesus I had read about stepped out of the pages of the Bible, and out of heaven, in the form of the Rock Church.

It was a refreshing reality, because when you are in prison over 10 years, family and friends get tired of the experience. After 20 years, they have moved on with their lives. The phone calls are few. The packages become Christmas-only. Kids become parents, parents become grandparents and pass on. So most of us inmates have become family for each other. But then God moved Pastor August into my life to refine my service and refresh my attitude. He brought the Agape Love that broken men need but run from. I look back on my journey—how selfish and foolish I was as a youth, and how committed I am now. The loyalty of the streets has been transferred to Christ Jesus and the Body of Christ.

Is this my testimony? A glimpse. When I think about my crime, I realize that I let the Enemy use me. So now I use each day to save a life in any way that Christ allows.

Do what u do Dean. Thanks! Brewster [smiley face drawn].

Baby sheep

> *Then Jesus told them this parable: "Suppose one of you has a hundred sheep and loses one of them. Does he not leave the ninety-nine in the open country and go after the lost sheep until he finds it?"*
>
> *Luke 15*

[The front door of the chapel at Donovan Prison faces out onto a large open yard used by the inmates. The chapel also has a small administrative office which can be used by the presiding clergyman.]

Right now I have a lot of baby sheep in the chapel—young gangbangers who have turned their lives over to Christ. A while back, their big homeys started coming into the chapel and those youngsters saw that, so they came in too. Now they are in the chapel, and they are hungry.

I love to go get those young gangbangers when they are out in the yard. I know how to go get them, because I have walked their walk. I know how their mind is set. I'll stand out in front of the chapel, watching the yard, and I'll see a youngster. I won't even know him, but I'll yell at him, "Hey man! Come over here!" and he'll come over.

I'll ask him, "What's your name?" and he'll tell me his name. Then I'll ask him, "Are you from San Diego?"

"Yeah, I'm from San Diego."

"What church does your daddy go to?" and he'll say such-and-such church.

Then I'll invite him into the chapel. "Come in the chapel here. I need to talk to you."

I get him in my office. And once I get him in my office and shut that door, it's on! It's a done deal! I tell him, "Man, I show movies in the chapel here, I do Bible studies, I do counseling." Finally I'll ask him, "This is your first time in prison, ain't it?"

"Yeah."

"You need someone to talk to."

"Yeah."

"You need to talk to me. I got some good stuff for you."

Before you know it, they're comin' in the chapel regular. I deal with the Hispanics and the Whites about the same way. Even the Skinheads, I say to them, "Come here, man! Let me talk to you!" and they come right over. It's just a gift that God has given to me. I know how to get those guys—the ones that are trying to be gangbangers, trying to run the street, trying to be bullies. I know how to reach out and get 'em—hands on!

Roscoe's House of Chicken 'n Waffles

The LORD said to Moses, "I have heard the grumbling of the Israelites. Tell them, 'At twilight you will eat meat, and in the morning you will be filled with bread.'" That evening quail came and covered the camp,....

The people of Israel called the bread manna. It was white like coriander seed and tasted like wafers made with honey.

Exodus 16

I am helping my twin daughters right now, because they're getting ready for the prom. And that has been making me reminisce about them. All the years that they have been teenagers, I have been here in San Diego and they have been up there in Long Beach. I go up there to be with them about every other weekend.

There's a place up there called Roscoe's House of Chicken 'n Waffles. Every time I go to Long Beach, my daughters say, "Dad, let's go to Roscoe's

House of Chicken 'n Waffles for breakfast!" The first time I went there, I said, "Chicken and waffles? I never heard of that combination." But I found out—it's good stuff! So when I go up to Long Beach to see my girls, I have to get ready for Roscoe's House of Chicken 'n Waffles.

Recently I was back down here in San Diego, preparing a sermon for the inmates in the prison. God had me titlelize the sermon, "Food for Your Soul," because I was thinking of the Bible as the original "soul food," you know? And as I was working on that sermon, I was thinking about Roscoe's. I thought, *Hmm. Where did they get that idea for putting chicken and waffles together?* Then the Lord said to me, *Well, I think Roscoe's got that idea from Me. I was serving that combination back in Biblical days*, and the Lord took me to the book of Exodus where it says, "That evening quail came and covered the camp,...." Well, I realized that's like chicken—you know, if you ate one bird, you ate 'em all!

Then the Lord showed me the next part where it says, "The people of Israel called the bread manna. It was white like coriander seed and tasted like wafers made with honey." Well, that's waffles and syrup right there! So I said, *Lord, you really DID make chicken and waffles back then!* I was so amazed. Later I showed that to my daughters and they said, "Dad, you're crazy."

Anyway, every time I go up to Long Beach to enjoy my daughters, we go out for chicken 'n waffles.

Dangerous Caprice

When we hear God and we listen to God, that will work for us, because when you do that, you are up under His divine protection. But when you step out and do your own thing, then you are only up under your own protection.

To show you what I mean, after I started doing prison ministry, God sent me from San Diego to Long Beach on a mission, to get together with some pastors; so I was on a mission for Him. If I was just up there messing around—just hanging out—I could have gotten killed.

There had been a lot of killings up in my old neighborhood among the gangs, and one of my little homeboys had just got killed. So some pastors in Long Beach had set up a time for me to come up and speak at a church. I went up there, took my daughters to Roscoe's House of Chicken 'n Waffles, and then met with those pastors. We met for an hour and then spent a half-hour in prayer.

Before going back to San Diego, I stopped at my cousin's house, because earlier I had seen a big crowd out in front of her house. It was all my young homeboys and homegirls that had just come from the funeral for that one homeboy that had got killed. They were all happy to see me, so I went into the house. They were all in there eating and talking.

While I was inside the house, one of the guys from the other gang came driving down the street outside. Some of our guys stopped him and snatched him out of his car and started beating and stomping him. Somebody ran in the house and said, "They're stomping on that guy out there!" I did not want to get into that stuff, so I was thinking, *I'm gettin' out of here.* But somehow the guy got away.

I talked to my cousin's mom a little while longer and then got ready to leave. I got into my van to leave and drove down the street, to a stop sign at a cross street. When I pulled up to that stop sign, on my left—coming towards me on the cross street—was a white Chevy Caprice. Then that Caprice made a right turn and pulled up next to my van and stopped. Four guys jumped out, and one them was that guy that had got beat up. He jumped out of the backseat on the driver's side, so he was right there by me. He stood there facing me with a gun in his hand, and I could see that my little homeboys had beat him real bad. Then he pointed that gun right at me, but I was stuck at the stop sign waiting for the crossing traffic. Then I heard, *click...click...click*, and I knew that he was really trying to kill me!

Right about then I got a chance with the crossing traffic, so I just punched it and made it across the intersection. Then I heard, *BOOM! BOOM! BOOM!* My van didn't have any air conditioning, so my windows were rolled down and I could hear the bullets whizzing past—*shizzzz, shizzzz, shizzzz*—so I kept driving. I drove down to the next corner and I heard more shooting, in the distance—*boom-boom,...boom-boom-boom.* That was my little homeboys who were back at the house, shooting at the guys in the white Caprice. They had seen them pull up next to me.

I was okay. But right away the Lord told me, *You're done with your work. Now you get out of here,* because the Lord knew that all I had to do was say a word to my little homeboys and that dude's head would be tooken off! The Lord didn't want me back around there. He said, *Well?* and I headed back to San Diego.

I had looked straight down the barrel of that gun. I saw that it was pointed straight at me! And on the way back to San Diego, the Lord brought something to my attention.

The Lord told me, *His gun got stuck.*

I said, "Man, Lord! Yeah."

The Lord told me, *Yeah, automatics—they stick like that.*

But then I thought for a minute, and I said, "Lord, that was a *revolver!*"

And that sure enough *was* a revolver! I could tell, because I looked right down the barrel. It was a six-shot revolver—like a Python or a 357 Magnum—and they don't stick!

I am amazed at how God protects us when we are about His business. It's so important that we stay about the Father's business instead of trying to do our own thing, because God is the one that really protects us. He's the one that leads us and guides us and instructs us.

So that day I sent word to the leader of the other gang, for him to handle things. I called one of my own homeboys and said, "Tell him that the guy shot at me when I was up there." I think he ended up reprimanding him, or something. He told me later that he took care of it. Even though he was from the other gang, we communicated and worked it out.

What happened?

We all have issues. Suppose you have an issue with your old spouse—maybe it was infidelity. Or suppose you are in prison on a drug issue. You have to deal with those issues. Otherwise you will take those issues from one situation to another, even hurting your intimate relationships.

Here's what happened with an inmate I knew. His name was Mohammed. I met him on Yard 3 at Donovan Prison, when I was the pastor on that yard. He was a big ol' dark-skinned guy. When I met him, he was getting out of prison soon, after doing ten years.

I really liked Mohammed. We talked about how we might hook up on the outside and do homeless ministry. But one time, I asked Mohammed, "What're you in here for?"

"Uh—drugs."

I said, "Alright. Cocaine? Heroin?"

"Heroin."

Then I asked Mohammed, "Have you dealt with that?"

He said, "What do you mean?"

"Have you dealt with that issue?"

"Well, I've been locked up for ten years."

I said, "But what about the drugs?"

"I ain't used drugs here in prison."

Then I told Mohammed, "Listen, bro'. By you bein' here incarcerated, you don't use drugs no more, and that's good. But there is still an issue here.

You need to address that issue. You need to make up your mind that you're goin' to get into a program when you get out of here."

"Naw. The dope—I dealt with that."

"How'd you deal with it? How'd it become a dead issue?"

"Man, I just ain't used drugs in here."

I told him, "What I'm tryin' to get across to you is that the issue is still there. Once you get out of this place and you get around your old homeboys in the old neighborhood, that will ignite the issue again."

"Naw. I got it handled."

I said, "Alright, bro'."

When Mohammed got out of prison, I had him coming to the parole officers' meeting as a motivational speaker, I had him coming to Bible studies, and I was just using him in different churches. He was on fire!

But that drug issue—the one he never dealt with—was still there. Mohammed's wife called me one day. She said, "August, Mohammed hasn't come home."

"What?"

"It's been a week."

I told her, "Let me find him."

I knew that Mohammed loved being downtown, so I just drove around down there, trying to find him. After about a week of driving around like that, I never saw him.

Then I went up to northern California to a prison chaplain's conference. Mohammed's wife called me there and asked me, "August, did you hear anything?"

I said, "Naw."

"Well, he wiped out the bank account."

"What?"

"He took all the money."

I told her, "I'm gonna ask questions."

So when I got back to San Diego, I spent the whole weekend looking around everywhere for Mohammed. On Monday morning, instead of going to the church office, I went downtown to try again. I couldn't find him, so I went straight from there to the prison. When I got there, two inmates walked up to me. One said, "Did you hear about Mohammed?"

"No. What happened?"

"Overdosed, in a hotel."

I thought, *Wow! It was that drug issue.*

Whenever I'm talking to a group of men, I ask them, "How many of you are in a relationship that is new, and some old relationship has left you with unresolved issues?" They all raise their hand. Then I tell them, "That old relationship left you with un-dealt-with issues, and you take those issues from that old relationship and bring them into the new one, and that new relationship doesn't stand a chance! It'll never work, because every time you're with your new spouse, you're still with that old spouse. Those un-dealt-with issues are still there. When you're layin' with your new spouse, you're still layin' with the old spouse; you bring the old spouse right into bed; you bring your old spouse right to the dinner table. In this new relationship, you're going to find yourself confronted with old issues you have that were never dealt with, with old issues that have nothin' to do with this new spouse, and that new spouse will go through hell with you! You're dealin' with— you're gettin' even with—that old spouse. So deal with those issues. Come to a conclusion. Come to an understanding. Come to a point of resolution! Or else it's always going to be a problem."

So we can't allow un-dealt-with issues. That's why Jesus told us in Mark, "When you stand praying, if you hold anything against anyone, forgive him, so that your Father in heaven may forgive you your sins." Jesus is saying, he knows that you have issues with that old relationship—call that other person's name out to him in prayer. That doesn't mean that you have to go looking for that person to try to resolve the matter, because you might not ever see that individual again or that individual might not receive your forgiveness because they are so messed up. Jesus is not telling you to go chase them down. But he is saying—when you pray, forgive.

That's how we deal with issues. Otherwise it will be a problem for us. That's why a lot of guys end up going back to the penitentiary. They have some issues that they never dealt with. They have an issue—of burglarizing, or of using drugs, or of spousal abuse—that they never actually dealt with. They know it's there. But actually dealing with it—overcoming the problem, manhandlin' the problem—they never did that. So it's a stumbling block for them.

I learned from experience that we need to deal with issues. Deal with them! Capitalize on them! Bring them to a halt! You know what I'm sayin'?

At the rescue mission

[Hunter often visits a men's rescue mission in downtown San Diego, to preach there.]

I went to the rescue mission Thursday night, and it was full of new guys. I saw one guy there that I knew from back at the prison chapel, a tall White guy we called Country. Country has got no front teeth, but he loves Jesus. Back when he was in prison, I told Country about the rescue mission, so when he got out of prison he got himself into the rescue mission, and he is doin' good!

I said, "Country, what do you do here?"

He said, "Pastor, when the men come in here, I greet 'em."

I said, "Boy, you're a servant!"

"Well, you taught us to be a servant."

Then it came time for me to preach. I had prepared a message about patience, but God said, *We're going to deal with this: My love.*

So I stood up and preached to those guys. I told them, "Some of y'all came in here with a backslidin' state of mind. You came in here to get cleaned up so you could go right back out there and do more drugs. You already got your mind made up. The Devil's convinced you that this is the way. So you come walkin' in here to be a failure." I could see that a lot of those guys got hit hard by that.

I kept going. "Now, God already knows that. He already knows what you're tryin' to do. But God don't want you to fail. Man, God has uniquely and wonderfully shaped us! He created us! He breathed life into us! He wants you to succeed!" I knew I was reaching them.

I said, "Don't you want your kids to be proud of you? Don't you want to be in a position to do good things for your kids, to make your kids proud that you are their dad? And don't you want to love and care for your wife? Don't you want to be respected as a man of God?" You could hear a pin drop. Some of them started to cry.

I shared how God has a purpose for them. "God has a purpose for each of you. Your job is to get into a personal relationship with God, so that He can reveal that purpose. And when you find that purpose, your life will be so compatible with that purpose that you won't have any problems fulfilling it. You can straighten out right now—by participating in the program here, by taking advantage of this program, by getting healed through this program— because God is in this program! You get chapel six nights a week here. You got all these different churches bringing Jesus in here. You can do it!"

And I preached to them about praise and worship. "You don't just worship God in music. You worship God—you praise Him—in everything you do. If it's no more than sitting down and writing, that's praise and worship. Everything you do, you can worship God in it. You can worship

Him in that thing. You can praise Him in that thing. You can invite Him into everything you do. And God loves it when we invite Him in, because He's a gentleman. He won't kick in the door. He'll knock on the door, but He's going to wait until you invite Him in. He won't come in if you don't want Him there."

Then I finished up. I said, "You guys need to be broken. *I* needed to be broken. I needed to be broken three or four times. When you're broken, that means God has stripped you of all material things—He takes everything away. He breaks your spirit so that He can give you the right spirit when He puts you back together again. There ain't no sense in God fixin' what's not broken! So you need to be broken first. God needs to break you so that you can mean something to the Kingdom of God, so that you can be worthy of a calling. You know what I'm saying? But until you're broken, you'll never mean *nothin'* to the Kingdom of God! Until you're broken, you are a friend to this world. And the Bible says that when a man is a friend to this world, he's an enemy of God. You've got to be a lover of God. You can't be a friend to this world. No, no, no!"

Man, I dealt with them for an hour. They were receptive. All I did was share God's love.

Billy, Rick and Pony

[Rick Slaton was a fearsome White inmate at Donovan Prison, whose cellmate was Billy Phillips. *Kairos* is an organized ministry that brings an intense three-day program into prisons.]

I remember when I first met Rick Slaton. He was the leader of the Skinheads on the yard. I talked with him and I looked at him and I listened to him. His own gang members respected him, but I knew that the Mexican Mafia also respected him highly—and the Crips and the Bloods too.

It was the way he carried himself. Talking to Rick, I thought, *There is something unique about this guy. There's good stuff about him.*

Billy and Rick were cellmates, and Billy would always read his Bible in his cell, and Rick saw that. Then Billy convinced Rick to come to *Kairos*. When Rick came to *Kairos*, he was quiet. And during *Kairos*, we brought Rick into my office. We ministered to him there and he accepted Christ. After *Kairos*, we scheduled Rick to be baptized. We planned on baptizing Rick together with a guy in his gang they called Pony. Rick had ministered to Pony after *Kairos*, and Pony wanted to get baptized too.

On the day of the baptism, I was waiting in the chapel. We had some other inmates that were ready to be baptized, but Rick and Pony hadn't shown up yet. I was worried. I was thinking, *I hope they didn't back out.* You know? But before long, Rick and Pony came walking through that chapel door in their prison shorts, with their towels—they were ready to get baptized! It was an amazing thing, because Rick was the leader of this big gang on the yard—the Whites, the Skinheads—and we baptized him and Pony.

Rick became a regular in the chapel. Every time something would take place in the chapel, Rick was there to sit and participate. He would come in and he would hear the message. Sometimes he got rapped across the wig by the message, but Rick never stopped comin'.

It is a blessing to see what God does when you are obedient. If you are obedient, God can work through your life. God will have you lead people to Him, people that you think would never listen. When you are obedient, you are operating out of the right spirit. You are operating out of the Holy Spirit. The Holy Spirit is leading you, guiding you, strengthening you—directly. That is why it is so important that we be obedient, that we do it the way God says to do it. That way, everything is going to work. Jesus told his disciples, "Go into town and you'll see a man with a pitcher of water. Ask him about a room for Passover." Jesus' disciples were obedient and went into town and saw the man with the pitcher of water and told him what Jesus had said, and the man said, "It's upstairs." It *worked* for them to be obedient. So when God gives us instructions, we have to do it His way. And when we do it His way, we come out way ahead. It works.

The team at the Rock

> [Hunter's efforts benefit from a prison ministry support
> team made up of members of the Rock Church, San Diego,
> California. Team members Christine, Paul, Robin, Darryl,
> Danielle and Teresita contributed the following.]

Christine

I know now that God can dwell inside prison walls. I never feel danger there. He surrounds the prison chapel with safety.

The inmates love and respect us volunteers. We sit next to them and pray and sing. I spent one Christmas inside Donovan. I found out that Christmas means forgiveness.

Paul

When I met August I thought he was a menacing character. Now I know he is the voice of reason. He encourages me to study harder. When I go to the prison, he meets me at the entrance like a big brother, making sure I am prayed-up and prepared. At this point I can truly minister to inmates who are serving double-digit sentences. I can visit them cell-to-cell if I have to.

The inmates respect August. He shows us how men should act.

Robin

By 2009, my own son had been transferred from Donovan State Prison to California Rehabilitation Center-Norco. He kept begging me to visit him there. But I felt overwhelmed by his six-year battle with crystal meth, and I could not break out of my *own* depression. I vowed not to go in that place—to walk under those guard towers and through that razor wire. But later on, I somehow agreed to attend a *Kairos* closing ceremony at Donovan, where (I was told) about 40 of Donovan's inmates would celebrate together with outsiders, after three days of Bible study.

I went. I got goose bumps walking through Donovan Prison. My heart raced faster and faster as each gate slammed behind me with a hard *CLANG!* I thought, *I don't want to be here.*

We sat down in the prison chapel and then clapped as the 40 men filed in, all dressed in their prison blues. A bald-headed inmate with a long red beard and tattoos everywhere got up to speak, and we could see he meant business. The other inmates followed. Each man was a glimpse of my son. I reached for a box of Kleenex that had been placed there. I couldn't breathe. I thought, *I need to leave!* but I was locked in there with them.

The next week I visited my son. The fear was gone. I was ready.

Darryl

One Sunday I was sitting in the prison chapel and I saw Earl raise his hand for permission to speak to the other inmates. A Black man in his forties, Earl stood up from his chair. He told us about the time he found his father's house and rang the doorbell, but his father said, "Boy! I don't owe you *nothin'!*" Earl's words stabbed me. After that Sunday, I watched Earl whenever I visited the chapel.

Danielle

[Danielle visits San Diego's juvenile jail.]

I have lived a sheltered life. So I was surprised when the kids I met in jail nodded their heads and raised their hands. I just met the youngest kid I have ever seen in jail—a 9 year-old. I spotted his baby-face amongst the 13-

17 year-olds who were sitting there. He sat quiet. Another boy asked me, "Do you guys come here every week?"

Teresita

The first time I walked into a prison, it was to visit my husband. I came in through the prison sally port and a guard let me through. I was afraid and unsure, but I really wanted to see him.

About three years after that I entered another prison, this time as a chapel volunteer at Donovan. We walked through the prison on a sidewalk parallel to the one used by families who were there to visit, separated from them by a chain link fence. Through that fence I saw women and children being processed and walking to visits with their men. The women looked anxious; the children seemed excited. I could remember my own pain.

Their biggest fear

I talk to the inmates before they get out of prison to go home. I ask them, "What is your biggest fear about gettin' out and goin' home?" I ask them that because fear can be a giant in your life. And if your fear becomes a giant in your life, then you have to become like David and become a giant-slayer. You know, David slew Goliath. And after David slew the giant, he cut off his head! We have to be a giant-slayer when it comes to our fears. We have to face them and conquer them.

When I ask the inmates "What is your biggest fear?" a lot of them talk right away about their relationship with their wife. It's amazing how for some of these guys—the toughest, meanest guys you can find, willing to tear a guy's head off his body—their biggest fear is a little-bitty, petite, beautiful wife. She's able to break him all the way down. It's amazing!

Don't be wavery

> *But let him ask in faith, nothing wavering. For he that wavereth is like a wave of the sea driven with the wind and tossed.*

James 1 (King James Version)

Always operate out of faith. Because, when you operate out of faith you can stand for God. You do not waver. You are not a wavery person. You cannot be a wavery person when you are working for God.

When you are wavery, you are not *solid* in your faith. You are compromising and soft and passive. You believe God in some areas of your life but not in others. A wavery-minded man is unstable in all his ways. He is straddling the fence. He is driven by the wind and tossed—and God ain't goin' for that!

So you can't be wavery. It is so important that you stand on your faith and you don't be wavery and you just be *solid* in your faith. The Devil tries to mess with you and tries to get you off of your faith, so that you are wavery and miss the whole lesson that God is trying to get over to you through your situation.

You can't play with God. I can't even *stand* to be around someone who plays with God, you know? I look to God for everything—I look to God for protection, I look to God for healing, I look to God for deliverance. For everything, you know? You can't be playin' both sides.

Big Chuck

> *I will remove from them their heart of stone and give them a heart of flesh.*

Ezekiel 11

When I first met Big Chuck in prison, he was a known-inmate out on the yard—mean as a junkyard dog! He was five hundred pounds of angry hate! He was like a Mack truck! He was a train locomotive! Italian yet.

For three years, I just watched Chuck. He would never speak to me. I would sometimes walk the yard or the housing units. Whenever I spotted Chuck, I would say, "Hey! How you doin'?" He would snarl at me and keep moving. I thought that was funny.

I would look at Chuck and think, *Just imagine getting him into the chapel!* That thought would actually pass through my head. But I didn't think that God was really going to call me on it.

One day when I saw Chuck, the Lord told me, *I want him.*

I thought, *Him, Lord?*

Yes.

Lord, why him?

I want him.

Why do You always give me the hard ones, Lord?

The other inmates knew that Chuck was mean and ruthless. They were saying, "No, no, no. Pastor won't get Big Chuck. That ain't *never* gonna happen!" They told me, "Pastor, you're not gonna get *him*." I said, "I'll get him," because the God I serve is bigger than twelve thousand Big Chucks.

It turned out, it was the easiest thing in the world to get him. When Chuck first came into the chapel, he wouldn't even talk to Blacks, because he was still full of hate and anger. But then I got Chuck into my office. I had a microwave oven in there and I cooked him a slice of pizza. He hadn't had pizza in years. Chuck ate the pizza and he opened up to me. We started talkin' and sharin'. All the other inmates were blown away!

After Chuck had been coming into the chapel for a while, I told him that he should lead the praise and worship part of our services. I knew Chuck had all this bad stuff bottled up inside of him for a long time. He never allowed anyone to get close to him, to open up and empty out. I knew that doing praise and worship would be like a pressure valve for Chuck—it would release all that pressure, all that anxiety, all that frustration. But Chuck told me, "Pfff. You must be crazy! I would never do that." I liked that reaction, because that's what *I* felt when John Leeder asked me to come into prison ministry.

Before long, Chuck was up there in front of the inmates doing praise and worship in the chapel. He loved it. He would put his heart into it. He could play the guitar. Aw, he could play that guitar! He could *play!* He would have that chapel rockin' and rollin'.

Chuck led the praise and worship in that chapel for a long time. But then it got to be a problem. Chuck was doing praise and worship, but he was still coming into the chapel bein' nasty, cussing, wanting to be the center of things. So I sat him down from praise and worship for a while. That devastated him. He was mad! But I was fighting for Chuck's soul. God wanted that boy to be right with Him. So I sat him down for a while. After he started again, Chuck told me, "Pastor August, by you taking a stand, that saved me."

Things went on from there. Hurricane Katrina happened in New Orleans. On about the second or third day of that, Chuck came into the chapel. He sat down in my office to talk to me.

Chuck said, "Pastor, shut the door." Then he hung his head.

I shut the door, I sat down, and I could tell he had been crying. I said, "What's goin' on?"

"I can't take it no more!"

"What can't you take, Chuck?"

"All this stuff on TV. How can they let that happen to those people?"

Chuck had been watching all the people being trapped by Hurricane Katrina. And now, in my office, he was crying like a baby. We stayed in there about forty-five minutes. My office door was closed, but I could hear some of the other inmates outside asking, "What's going on in there?" Others were saying, "He's got Chuck in there." Some guys knocked on the door to see what was happening, because they couldn't believe it.

Chuck kept asking me how they can let that stuff happen to those people in New Orleans. He told me that he can't hate anymore, that the hate is being drawn out of him, that his heart is getting real tender. I explained to Chuck how God was dealing with him, how God was taking out his heart of stone and giving him a heart of flesh, how God was letting him know that he is human. I explained how God was instilling love in him, and that the Katrina thing was just the reaction to that. I told him, "You can't stand to see anyone abused." He told me that now hate makes him sick to his stomach and that he can't do it anymore.

God peeled Chuck like a banana in that office. And after He peeled him, I could see a man that needed love, and needed someone that he could open up to. I had to be there for him. I came to realize that Chuck was one of the nicest persons you could ever meet. But he had a thing about being big. He had that body on him. He didn't want people around him. So he would put on a show—that he was a hater, that he was evil, that he was a racist. But in all that, he was really crying out for help. He needed to share what was on his heart. You know, if you don't share that stuff, that stuff will kill you.

Chuck and I went through a lot in prison. He knew I loved him. He knew I cared about him. Chuck was my friend.

When Chuck got out of prison, I found out that I was the only friend he had. He would call me in the middle of the night. He would call me every day, and we would talk. I would set things up for him to help me. I wanted him to feel important. I'd say, "Chuck, I need you to help me deal with this one guy I know," and he would help me. Sometimes I would have the Rock Church cut him a check, because he wasn't doing good for money. So we really connected after he got out of prison.

I had told Chuck when he was in prison, "When you get out, we're going to this place I know and eat lunch. You'll like this place."

He said, "Oh yeah?"

So I asked him, "Chuck, what's your favorite thing to eat?"

"I like to eat steaks!"

I said, "Aw fine. This place will work out just beautiful."

So right when he got out of prison, I took Chuck to this Brazilian steak house, downtown, over on Fourth Avenue. Oh my God, this place is something! Before you order your steak, they have all these side dishes in a buffet, off to the side—real elegant, real nice. Then, at your table, they give you this little device made out of wood. It's shaped like an hour glass and one end is painted green and the other end is red, and when you want the waiter to bring more steak you turn the green side up, and when you want them to stop for a while you turn up the red side. And they bring different types of steak to your table. It comes right off the grill on a skewer, and they bring it and slice it off the skewer for you, right at your table. Every type of steak you can name, they have it—plus ham with pineapples in it, chicken covered in cheese, turkey, even Italian sausage. And they give you as much as you want.

So me and Chuck were sitting in there eating and I was just amazed at Chuck. I said, "Chuck! You done ate a whole cow, brother!" That restaurant loves when they get someone in there that can really eat. But after a while, I thought they were going to put us out, because Chuck was really packin' it away. The steak just kept comin' and comin', and we kept talkin'. One time Chuck pushed his hands at me and told me, "August, you're talkin' too much. Let me chew up some of this steak," and I said, "Okay, brother." We sat there for hours. That brother just ate steak and steak and steak and steak. He said, "Man, it's been years since I been able to eat like this." I said, "Well, don't hurt yourself, man!" We had a ball. I remember that like it was yesterday, because me and Chuck had been through a lot.

But Chuck really wanted to lose weight. He wanted to have that surgery where the doctor puts a band—like a gasket—around part of your stomach. He had been talking about it to me and Becky over the phone. He had medical insurance and he was getting money in from the county. So Becky checked a few places about the surgery, but nobody would accept his insurance. We finally found one doctor who would do the gasket on him.

When we told Chuck to call this doctor and set up an appointment, he was excited! He got scheduled for a Wednesday visit, and the surgery was the Friday after that. Chuck told me, "Aw Pastor. When I get this surgery, I'm going to lose a lot of weight. I won't be just 'Chuck.' I'll be 'Sexy Chuck!'" Becky and I laughed real hard at that. He was so excited. This was something he wanted his whole life, to be able to lose weight. He was over five hundred pounds. He said, "Man, I'm actually going to have the surgery after all these years."

But then Big Chuck died the Saturday before. It was Chuck's mom that told me. She said, "Chuck passed Saturday." I was blown away. She said, "I had to call you because you are all Chuck talked about. My son loved you. He always talked about Pastor Hunter this, Pastor Hunter that." I told her I was coming up to LA to meet her.

So me and Becky went to see Chuck's mom. We were in Long Beach for Thanksgiving, so we made a plate of food for Chuck's mom and drove to LA. We spent some hours with her. She lives by herself. She told us all about Chuck. Chuck was abused by her boyfriend when Chuck was a little boy. She said that gave Chuck his angry attitude.

Then Chuck's mom told us about how Chuck died. Chuck had this homeless friend that he was taking care of, in downtown LA. The Saturday that Chuck died, the weather was real cold, so Chuck went and got his friend and bought him some food and got him a room so that his friend didn't have to sleep on the street that night. She told us that the two of them sat there in the room and ate. The friend was sitting at a table and Chuck was sitting on the bed and they were watching a football game on TV. Then Chuck laid back on the bed and went to sleep. The friend told his mom that Chuck was talking just before Chuck went to sleep and that Chuck fell asleep while he was talking, so he didn't bother Chuck; he just let Chuck sleep and kept watching the football game. Later Chuck's friend tried to wake Chuck up, but he wouldn't wake up. He was dead.

When Chuck died, that messed me up so bad. Chuck was just getting ready for his surgery. He was all excited. He wanted to be Sexy Chuck. I wanted to *see* Sexy Chuck. I remembered how in prison, God had me fighting for Chuck. The Devil wanted that brother. But God wanted Chuck, so He had me to help him. I miss that brother.

I didn't know God was going to take that boy home like that. I see now that God wanted Chuck ready before he got out of prison. When Chuck died, I felt like God was telling me, *Well, he ran his race. It was time for him to come home with Me*. It made me realize that my job was over and that we don't have to force things to happen once our job is over.

The night Chuck died, his friend called the police and they investigated things. A lot of people, when they first heard that Chuck had died, said, "Aw—probably drugs involved." I was getting angry with that. I waited for the autopsy report to come back, because Chuck's mom had asked me to find out why Chuck died. When I finally read the autopsy report, it listed "obesity," and something about Chuck's heart. Yeah, I remember—it said something about Chuck's heart. There was no drugs involved.

The love chapter

If I speak in the tongues of men and of angels, but have not love, I am only a resounding gong or a clanging cymbal.

If I have the gift of prophecy and can fathom all mysteries and all knowledge, and if I have a faith that can move mountains, but have not love, I am nothing.

If I give all I possess to the poor and surrender my body to the flames, but have not love, I gain nothing.

Love is patient, love is kind. It does not envy, it does not boast, it is not proud.

It is not rude, it is not self-seeking, it is not easily angered, it keeps no record of wrongs.

Love does not delight in evil but rejoices with the truth.

It always protects, always trusts, always hopes, always perseveres.

Love never fails. But where there are prophecies, they will cease; where there are tongues, they will be stilled; where there is knowledge, it will pass away.

1 Corinthians 13

It says, "If I speak in the tongues of men and of angels, but have not love, I am only a resounding gong or a clanging cymbal." In other words—you are talkin' loud and sayin' nothin'!

And it says, "If I have the gift of prophecy and can fathom all mysteries and all knowledge, and if I have a faith that can move mountains, but have not love, I am nothing." See, we are *nothing* without love! To mean anything to the Kingdom of God, we have to operate out of love, because that is the very nature of God. That is why Jesus put so much emphasis on love— "Love your neighbor as yourself," and "Love the Lord your God with all your heart, mind, soul and strength."

It says, "If I give all I possess to the poor and surrender my body to the flames, but have not love, I gain nothing." So we are nothing without love.

Then comes the real meat. It says love is patient. That means love is long-suffering. Love is willing to go a long ways with you. I have been going a long ways with my dad, even though he has done all these things to me, ever since I was a kid. Man, I have been goin' a *long* ways with him.

And love is kind. Love doesn't operate out of just any type of character. Love is kind and gentle.

Love does not envy. That means, love is not looking at what you have that *it* doesn't have. Love is looking at what you have and is coming alongside you and saying, "God bless you!" Love is rejoicing over what you have, not coming against you for what you have. Love doesn't operate like that.

Love is not proud or all puffed up. Love's head is not swollen.

Love is not easily angered. So if I'm operating out of love, I am not letting myself be easily provoked by you. This love is a defense weapon. It not only helps you love people the way God wants, but it will protect you too.

Love does not delight in evil. Love is not thinking of ways it can hurt you. Love is thinking of ways it can bless you. Even though my dad does things to hurt me, I am not trying to figure out ways to hurt *him*. I am thinking of ways to bless him.

Love rejoices in the truth. So love is a friend, because only a friend will tell you the truth. I don't need someone to help kill me with a lie. I can do that by myself. I need someone to come alongside me and tell me the truth—that I'm wrong. Then I can get myself right.

Love protects, trusts, hopes and perseveres—there's that long-suffering again. Amen? No matter what you are going through—suppose someone is handling you rough, or someone is hurting you—you will be able to endure. Love has some tolerance. Love can bear some things. Love is willing to go through some things with you. Love allows you to go through things and still be able to maintain!

And then, love never fails. And that is what I love about God—there is no failure in Him, because God is love and love never fails.

When we love, we will not always be loved back. But God tells us, *Don't worry about that. Your job is to love. You be caught loving.* And this is where I am with my dad. Whether he loves me or not, I love him. Despite everything that went on in the past, I love him. That's the bottom line. Whether he loves me back—he will have to deal with God on that.

Chapter 7 Study Guide

Breaking into prison

When you have experienced something, you can truly help others who are going through that same experience. Experience allows us to really pull alongside people. Experience is why we can consider Christ to be our brother. He has been in this world, he has walked among us and lived as a human being, experiencing uncertainty, betrayal, suffering and relationships. His experience is what allows us to connect with him. What difficulty have you experienced that later became a blessing for others? How has someone else's difficult experiences been a comfort in your life, when they shared them with you?

Charley got out

Although God may try many things, it often takes suffering to wake us up. Sometimes, only when we suffer pain do we understand how skewed our perspective has gotten, or realize the loving plan that God has for us. Death sets us free from earthly pain, but we can avoid a great deal of it in this world by keeping our hearts and mind on God's word, and His work in our life. We are all invited to be freed by the truth. It's a choice. What pain could you have avoided in your life by staying focused on God's will in your life? If a bad choice has brought you pain, how has God restored you?

Brother C. Zachary Brewster, CIA man

God does indeed teach us that, "human identity is not a static state." The Bible gives us the entire story of human identity, capping the story off with the perfect character of Jesus. No matter how stuck we are in our lives—in a job, in a relationship, or in prison, either actual or virtual—God can surprise and refresh us, and we can grow to expect it. Are you somehow stuck and in need of refreshment? If so, are you hopeful, or have you given up on getting a parole date?

Baby sheep

We often meet individuals who are lost or misguided. And we can underestimate our ability to bring stability, encouragement and guidance into their lives. If we approach someone with the idea that we have something to give, rather than with a spirit of judgment and prejudice, we will be surprised by the response. We can be shepherds in a world full of confusion, danger and ignorance, but only if we reach out deliberately and lovingly to those in need. When, in your life, have you gained from someone reaching out to you generously and lovingly? How do you rate your ability to relate to strangers who may need your help or guidance?

Roscoe's House of Chicken 'n Waffles

God provides. He provides for us at the highest level, nurturing our spirit through His word and His work of salvation. But he also provides for us in a daily way, as he did for the children of Israel in the desert. He tells us not to worry, that He is aware of our daily needs. And we get—often enough—a good night's sleep, food to eat, shelter, the beauty of nature and arms to hug. It's all His provision. And He provides all those things so that we may love and enjoy each other and Him. When you are going through a hard time, are you able to focus on what God has already done for you and take comfort in that? What so occupies your mind that sometimes you overlook God's daily provisions?

Dangerous Caprice

It is not accurate to simply say that God protects those who are obedient and punishes those who are disobedient. But God does promote His purposes throughout our lives. And when we focus on God's purposes, we naturally align ourselves with His efforts and we sense His presence. Likewise, when we lose our focus on God's purposes, life becomes discordant. Part of God's loving nature is to help us regain that focus. Yet that may only occur after much pain and stress. Life is more exciting and much easier when we discern God's purposes in our life. This is what we would expect from a loving Father. Have you ever experienced protection that can't be explained in any ordinary way? Have you ever felt a nudging to go in a different direction when you have been headed down a particular path in life? Did you respond to the nudging or did you keep going down your path?

What happened?

In a courtroom, when a lawyer identifies the "issue," he or she is identifying the problem that needs to be resolved by the judge or jury. We use that word the same way in everyday life. If there is an unresolved issue in our life, it means that there is some unhealthy tension that will continue to hurt us. If the issue remains unresolved, the tension will persist and there will be an absence of peace in our lives. We need to deal with issues, so that there is greater peace in our lives. But when we ignore issues, their destructive impact continues. Do you view yourself as "issue-free" in life, or do your struggle with identifiable issues? If you still struggle with an issue, how can it be resolved?

At the rescue mission

Many of us go through life never expecting real change. We expect to stay on the same path in life, one that goes nowhere. The most we expect is to get "clean" for a while, before we move on and continue in the same way.

But God's love breaks through all that. It breaks the old pattern of our behavior. It excites our imagination about new ways of living. It provides hope for real change, in constructive directions. It adds genuine trust to our relationships with others. We get rescued. Are you living a routine life, without any real God-given adventure? Are you giving hope to those around you by exhibiting signs that God is at work in your life?

Billy, Rick and Pony

When we are open and obedient, God can use us. If we go through life willing to be led by God's loving Spirit, we won't be afraid to go into difficult situations or deal with difficult people. The burden of the moment isn't on us—what to do, what to say, how to be. God has already handled that. We are there to be a conduit of His truth and love.

Jesus was no different. What he accomplished was a reflection of his relationship with his Father, through openness and obedience. It was not the result of cleverness, personal power or charisma. He was genuinely connected to his Father, and miracles happened. What is it that blocks your personal openness and obedience to God? Have you had an experience of being God's conduit?

The team at the Rock

Prison walls do not truly separate us from the men and women behind them. There they remain human and continue to crave love and acceptance, as we do. If we know them personally, we may share their pain. If we don't know them, God would have us empathize. They live in a world we do not know or experience, and only the light of Christ can pierce such darkness. Are you too quick to judge those who are behind prison walls? Are you willing to visit—either actually or in spirit—those who are imprisoned?

Their biggest fear

What would cause an inmate to fear his wife? On the positive side, one cause could be the fear of being held accountable. On the negative side, it could be that the inmate is married to someone who is not good for them—someone who is unfairly demanding, negative, critical, authoritarian or rebellious. In dealing with fear, it is important to discern its cause. Is the fear caused by reality or by bad thinking? If fear is based in reality, then we need to take steps to guard our safety. If it is based on bad thinking, we need to stop frightening ourselves. If your fear comes from not trusting God, do you somehow think He is limited? What people in life cause you fear? How are you giving away your power in relation to those people?

Don't be wavery

Often when a person undertakes some change in life, they do well for a while. But then they are tested. Something—some event or some person—circles back through their life to test whether they will enter once more into old patterns of behavior. If they are wavery, progress is arrested and they are forced to start again. On the other hand, if they are "sold out" to God and His plan, He can change and direct them. They can avoid the distraction and move forward on a God-directed path. To be wavery minimizes God. It reduces our trust in what He can do. When were you near a success and fear took over? When you have operated in a wavery fashion, how did you distort God and what He has said?

Big Chuck

Emotionally speaking, some people go through life like a giant porcupine. Their quills are up and ready to stab anyone who reaches out to them. So people stand back. Porcupines are not approachable.

But like the real ones, emotional porcupines have a soft underbelly. Their quills are often defending some special tenderness that was betrayed or wounded. Those people need someone brave and discerning enough to pet a porcupine, to get to the soft underbelly. For Big Chuck, that was August. We can be God's representative and reach out to touch the emotional porcupines we encounter. It was friendship, not surgery, that healed Chuck. What defense mechanisms have you developed to keep yourself safe? What hurt, pain or betrayal caused you to protect yourself? As safe as your defense mechanism seems to keep you, what is it actually costing you?

The love chapter

1 Corinthians 13 is popular at weddings. But it is profound, not just popular. Imagine how our daily lives would go if this chapter was our focus. It would change what we say, how we respond and what actions we take. That would make a huge difference for the children in many homes. Every home has an emotional environment. It takes only one person to wreck it. What verse in the love chapter did you experience most when you were young? What verse did you experience least from your parents? What verse do you have the most trouble with in your own life?

Notes